# A BULLETIN BUFFET

*to Lee
From Father Paul*

## Fr. Paul Prabell

Published by: Cathedral of Christ the King, Lexington, Kentucky.

Cover photograph by Maureen Guarnieri-Yeager
Interior photographs by Maureen Guarnieri-Yeager
Book & Cover design by Trang Baseheart

First edition, 2022

ISBN: 9798811643318
Imprint: Independently published

# TABLE OF CONTENTS

...ies is the social service ministry of the Diocese of Lexington with a mission to empower and assist individuals ...throughout the diocese to improve their quality of life. As a critical part of the safety net to our neighbors in ...lic Charities assists people of all races, beliefs, and backgrounds. Through the Bridging the Gap emergency program, Catholic Charities staff assists individuals and families experiencing a financial crisis by providing help ...utilities, food, diapers, and other essential items, as available. Catholic Charities was a key provider of pandemic ...rent assistance helping families to remain in their home and continues to help those who were evicted to relocate ...housing. When disasters such as floods or tornadoes strike, Catholic Charities stands ready to help and responds ...compassion and commitment. As the primary domestic disaster relief agency of our Diocesan Church, services after ...aster may assist with temporary shelter, supplies for home repairs, replacement of items lost, rent or utility assistance, ...d emotional support.

Meg Campos serves as the Executive Director of Catholic Charities. The agency currently has four staff members and is recruiting another to develop family programs for those served by the Centro de San Juan Diego, an apostolate of the diocese. Additionally, Catholic Charities is in the process of contracting counselors to offer in-person and telehealth counseling to those who lack insurance or otherwise couldn't afford such services. Additionally, all agency services are currently available in Spanish.

Throughout the pandemic, Catholic Charities has not held a fund-raising event or operated at a full staff level. As the staff and the board of directors are now growing and preparing to offer even more services, the needs for spiritual and financial support are growing. We encourage you to keep our mission in your prayers and to generously support the ministry of Catholic Charities. ....A first step could be to purchase a copy of Fr. Paul's book, A BULLETIN BUFFET. All of the proceeds will benefit Catholic Charities.

# INTRODUCTION

This compilation of bulletin columns from August 2015 to June 2021 are offered as one way of sharing the celebration of the 50th anniversary of my ordination to the priesthood. I am gratified that many parishioners found them to be helpful; in fact, so helpful that some have even read the bulletin while I was preaching.

As Father Ray Stratman lived with us at the rectory, he felt a sense of mission to enhance my humility. As a former high school teacher, and as one who worked crossword puzzles with an ink pen, he looked forward to obtaining a bulletin as soon as the printed copies arrived at the O'Neill Center and with red pen circling any misspellings, mistakes or typos. But he also offered some compliments on columns which he found interesting.

I have enjoyed writing these columns. I saw this weekly endeavor as one more way to minister to a large community with which I never was able to have enough person-to-person contact. The columns have varied as I have written about programs taking place in the parish, liturgical seasons of the year and feast days which were upcoming, theological and spiritual topics, and occasionally have shared a bit of my personal story. The years 2015–2021 were marked by our Capital Campaign, the payment of our prior debt and the many renovation projects, several changes and developments in our staff and their roles, our school receiving its second Blue Ribbon Award, and of course, by Covid-19. Throughout it all, my personal goal was to guide the diversity of our parish members to work together and to grow together as a community of disciples living with faith, hope and love.

Very often a column would begin with one topic and then evolve into another topic. That is how life is: one thing leads to the next, but it is somehow all related. That is why the title *A Bulletin Buffet* seems appropriate. A buffet offers many good choices. Hopefully, that is the case with this book. There are 50 chapters; that number has been stimulated by 50 years as a priest, but also with the thought that — with this introduction which you are reading and with the closing reflection, there can be food for spiritual nourishment for the 52 weeks of the year. Like all buffets, sometimes the chapter topics run into one another, just like the many enticing food items run together on a typical buffet plate. And like all buffets, there will be some offerings which will be more to your taste than others, some might be disappointing and some might taste better than you expected.

Over the years, we have been very proud of our bulletin. It has won national awards. In a way, our bulletin is like a parish magazine. I see it as an important aspect of our ministry. I am very grateful for all who contribute to its excellence and grateful for all the businesses whose ads sponsor the bulletin. I hope that you find this collection of bulletin columns to be a source of nourishment for your spirit.

*Father Paul Prabell*

# CHAPTER 1

*Beginning Again:*

BULLETIN — August 16, 2015

It feels very good and "right" to be returning to Christ the King as rector. I have been blessed throughout my priesthood because all of my assignments have been positive. I have grown with each parish and community, have facilitated some growth, and have felt at home in every assignment.

I have loved serving in Morehead and its surrounding mission areas. It was not an easy decision to transfer to Christ the King. Several Morehead parishioners experienced some grief, and I also had my share of grief in this process. But once I made the decision to say yes to Bishop John's request I was at peace, and that sense of peace has only deepened in the days since I have arrived here.

From 2002–2007, Christ the King and Lexington were my home. From 2008–2015, Jesus Our Savior Church and Morehead were my home. Now Christ the King is my home again. The title of Thomas Wolfe's 1940 novel, *You Can't Go Home Again* suggests an interesting paradox.

I have returned to a home...but neither the home nor I are the same. I know Christ the King's community, but I don't. Christ the King is the same...but different. Some people, programs, blessings, and challenges are the same...but there have been some changes. So too with me. I am the same but different. I am not simply your old rector (although my senior's discount status is being more quickly recognized at fast food restaurants).

There have been changes in all of us; hopefully the majority of these changes have been improvements. Yet there is a fundamental core to all of us and to our community. How the new and the old will intersect in our lives will be part of a wondrous adventure of walking with Our Lord as disciples.

And we are beloved disciples. We are called to learn more about Jesus and to share his life. We all need to feel at home but we are also called to share the life of Our Lord with those who at not at home with the ways their lives have developed. ♛

*Photo by Maureen Guarnieri-Yeager*

# CHAPTER 2

*Essence of a Parish:*

BULLETIN — December 6, 2015

BULLETIN — November 15, 2020

In his 2014 book, *Divine Renovation*, Father James Mallon emphasizes that a vibrant parish is not simply focused on maintaining its present status and programs. Rather, a vibrant parish focuses on its mission, the heart of which is leading each parishioner to live as a disciple of Jesus. To be a disciple means seeking to know Jesus, being in relationship with Jesus, and sharing in the work of Jesus. Father Mallon says parishioners need to be respected, accepted, and welcomed, but they also need to know what is expected of them. He refers to a parish brochure which outlines what parishioners can expect from their parish and what the parish expects of parishioners. As I present Father Mallon's thoughts, I will do so in a summary fashion...but I share these thoughts because they offer to all of us a challenge and a means of measuring the journey we share as a parish community.

Father Mallon's brochure names what parishioners have a right to expect of their parish...

- Dynamic and uplifting liturgies
- A place where you will experience transformation to become more and more the person God has created you to be
- A place where you will be valued and recognized as having unique gifts and talents for the service of God and others...and where you can use them.
- A place where you will be loved and supported in your spiritual journey regardless of the messiness and struggles of your life
- A place where your needs will be listened to and addressed
- A place where your input is valued
- A place where your financial contributions will be honored and put to work for the building up of the Kingdom of God with transparency and accountability

The brochure then proceeds to name what is expected of parishioners...

- We expect all members of the parish to gather for Sunday worship unless they are unable to do so because of illness or travel
- We expect all members of the parish to be dedicated to growth as a disciple and therefore to commit to at least one program of faith formation every year
- We expect all members to see themselves as part of a community of believers and therefore to reach out and to connect with parishioners in order to build community
- We expect every parishioner to be involved in at least one of the parish's ministries
- We expect all parishioners to give generously of their financial resources so that the parish can build up God's Kingdom. ♛

We are in the midst of our Stewardship Renewal Drive. I give thanks for all the folks who are offering witness talks this weekend. They are representative of so many of you who have a dedication to living your discipleship through the many ways of being givers. Thank you and thank you for the joy which accompanies that spirit of generosity...the joy is infectious and inspiring.

Next weekend is the culmination of our Capital Campaign. I am grateful for all who have made donations and pledges. It has been very successful. The number of parishioners who have been part of this campaign sets a record for our parish; that number states that you wanted to help our Church continue to be a home and haven for our community for years to come. The recent completion of our bell tower, spire and cross projects symbolizes who we are as a Church, but also symbolizes the spirit of our parish's response to this campaign to repair our church and its infrastructure and prepare for the future.

As we enter into a Stewardship Renewal Drive, the areas we are concerned with are: 1) financial giving; 2) volunteering your talents and 3) investing ourselves even more so in prayer.

1) Back in September when I spoke of our financial needs, I encouraged you to consider raising your offertory giving by 10 percent. I also encourage you, as you complete your pledge to our capital campaign, to continue contributing on that same level to our offertory.

2) We will be in drastic need of volunteers to join our ushering ministry, at least for our Christmas Eve and Christmas Day Masses. This will be a unique and dramatic year, as we will have reduced capacity and therefore several more Masses than our usual number of Christmas Masses. I know many folks love going to Christmas Mass with your family. I encourage you to do so...but also to come to another Mass to serve as an usher. That will be a great Christmas gift to Our Lord and to our community.

3) During these days of the pandemic, polarization and civic unrest, we all do well to invest ourselves even more deeply in petitionary prayer. When we humbly come to God and name what we hope for, God listens and we become connected even more intimately with God. We may see our requests granted, but we may not; however, our honesty with God changes us.

This week and last week I will have been in 11 meetings with church committees dealing with a variety of issues related to Church life. Most of these will be virtual meetings. The meetings always serve as a "think tank" as the committee members offer advice regarding important aspects of our parish's life. In addition to the guidance I receive for "guiding our lifeboat", committee meetings enable me to know many wonderful people and help the parish to know that the decision-making process on both large and small matters is a shared process.

75 years ago, Father O'Neill had his advisory committee of members of the parish as they chose the land for our church campus, as they projected the growth which would take place in the contemporary farmlands of Chevy Chase, as they convinced the Bishop that they needed to purchase the entire block rather than half of it, and as they worked out the financial arrangements for the loan of the money for our property.

75 years ago, on November 17, 1945, Christ the King parish purchased our property for $35,000!!! ⛪

# CHAPTER 3

*Monsignor O'Neill:*

BULLETIN — August 30, 2020

BULLETIN — September 20, 2020

It was on September 2, 1945 that Father Richard Garland O'Neill was appointed the pastor of Christ the King. When the parish was established, in the spring of that year, Fr. O'Neill had no idea he would be serving as the pastor. Yet as a native of Lexington and the son of a blacksmith, once appointed, Fr. O'Neill knew he could build on his many friends and relationships within the city and the horse industry in order to help the parish grow.

The first task was to develop membership, to develop a community of faith. The second task, closely related, was to generate the financial resources so the parish could build. It is striking that as we are in the midst of the pandemic, socially distancing, and seeing a small fraction of our regular members, we face similar challenges today...rebuilding our congregation and rebuilding our financial base. Just as Fr. O'Neill did not expect to be named a pastor (I believe this was his first time as a pastor), so we did not expect a pandemic to hit us.

I think it will be good to ask Fr. O'Neill to pray for us and to inspire us from his place in heaven.

Whenever we move, we bring our stuff with us. Our "stuff" includes our clothes and furniture but also our memories and our devotions. Father O'Neill certainly brought his devotions with him when he moved to Christ the King. And we see evidence of that in many of the art pieces throughout the cathedral.

Fr. O'Neill had a devotion to the Infant of Prague. Prayers inspired by the Eastern European devotion to the little boy Jesus are credited with preserving Catholic nations from the threat of oppression by rival anti-Christian nations. The Infant of Prague brought Fr. O'Neill great solace as he worried at times about the future of the Church and the parish's development.

Many people are curious about the array of saints in the stained glass windows on the walls on either side of the Church. St. Patrick is the saint of the Irish, but also the name of Fr. O'Neill's father; St. Catherine was a great spiritual teacher and an advisor to popes during a difficult time in church history. Catherine is also the name of Fr. O'Neill's mother. St. Richard de Wyche, also known as Richard of Chichester, was a 13th century British bishop, and Fr. O'Neill's patron saint.

Andre Bessette was a humble Canadian brother, a doorkeeper, whose holiness was so transparent that he was a spiritual director and confidant for many people. Miguel Pro was a priest in Mexico at a time when the church was being persecuted. Fr. O'Neill was in the seminary and his early years of priesthood when both Andre Bessette and Miguel Pro were living.

St. Anthony of Padua, a Franciscan priest, is the beloved patron of people who have lost something (or someone). Dismas is regarded as the name of the "Good Thief" and therefore gives testimony that all people are redeemable; St. John Vianney is the patron of parish priests.

St. Therese of Lisieux, the Little Flower, died in the late 19th century, and her spiritual writings have touched many people. John Martin Moye, was the founder of the Congregation of Divine Providence, religious sisters dedicated to education, especially focused on the children of poor families. Fr. O'Neill had served with them in Northern Kentucky and members of that religious order of women were the first faculty of our school.

We will commemorate the appointment of Fr. O'Neill as pastor and the beginning of the great adventure and mutual love affair between him and our parish with the 5:30 p.m. Mass on Wednesday of this week, followed by an ice cream social in Hehman Hall and our courtyard.

Even more so, we pledge to seek his prayers and intercession as we begin the next 75 years facing a great challenge. May his prayers join with those of many other saints as we rebuild our Church. May we all draw from his faith, vision and steadfastness as we move forward! ♛

This year we are observing the 75th anniversary of the founding of our parish. Our usual parish life has been extremely disrupted by the pandemic. As this year goes on and probably as we move into next year, in effect, we will be re-founding our parish (as will many churches throughout the world). We can learn from history. And so I offer 10 aspects of founding a parish as I imagine Fr. O'Neill in action back in 1945. (Many of you who have been in Lexington for some time can recall the formation of St. Elizabeth Ann Seton and Pax Christi parishes and can notice similarities in the process.)

1) We obtain some property. In September and October, 1945, Fr. O'Neill and his property committee were evaluating several tracts of land in the Chevy Chase area.

2) We create a worship space. Having Mass at St. Catherine's Academy was not enough. A pre-fabricated church building became the first worship space...but it was our space!

*Cathedral of Christ the King*

**Celebrating**

**75**

**years!**

3) The pastor meets the people of the community...walking the neighborhoods, meeting business leaders, going to stores and restaurants...listening to the people he meets, seeking to understand the concerns and hopes of the people for the area encompassed by the parish.

4) The pastor meets the Catholic people of the area and those who show interest in the emerging parish. He exudes kindness, compassion and interest in a way that shows his care is transparent.

5) The pastor observes the men and women who have the capacity to be leaders and develops committees who will advise him and who will reach out to others.

*1945-2020*

6) The pastor undertakes a process of evangelization. He and parish leaders reach out to those who are alienated, disenchanted or simply away from the Church; he listens and offers gentle invitations and wise explanations.

7) The developing community begins to generate a spirit of excitement; they realize that they are part of a wonderful adventure which will touch many lives and, in fact, will change many lives. For many of the early parishioners being part of this new parish becomes the center of their lives.

8) The pastor does a lot personally and also facilitates ministry to the sick, the poor, the troubled, and to children. A community of care begins to emerge.

9) The parishioners accept and build on and refine a dream for what the parish will be like when it is fully alive. This dream includes what the buildings will be like, but even more so what the soul of the parish will be.

10) A spirit of giving emerges. People are ready to give of themselves as volunteer workers, as idea people and as financial donors. Just like in a good family, because of love, sacrificial giving becomes the norm, so that the vision can become a reality.

And with every aspect, prayer is the foundation...liturgical prayer with daily Mass in some kind of make-shift chapel or worship space and the daily prayer of the pastor and the members of the parish community. "Unless the Lord build the house, they labor in vain who build it" (Psalm 127).

# CHAPTER 4

*Our School:*

BULLETIN — January 29, 2017

BULLETIN — August 13, 2017

Throughout this year, the Gospel passages for our Sunday Masses will primarily be excerpts from the Gospel of Matthew. More than any other Gospel, Matthew presents Jesus as a teacher. There is a pattern throughout this gospel. Jesus teaches and then he engages in deeds of ministry. There is a rhythm as the scenario repeats itself. Jesus teaches by his words, but he also teaches by example.

This week as we observe Catholic Schools Week, we celebrate our school, Lexington Catholic, and all the Catholic Schools in our Diocese. We acknowledge the many successful people whose educational, moral and spiritual foundations were laid here at Christ the King School.

Our school provides an exceptional education in every academic field. Our students are prepared to excel at the next level of education. Additionally, we focus on Christian values and virtues, have Religion classes as part of our day by day curriculum, prepare students to celebrate and live the sacraments, sensitize them to the importance of the works of mercy, engage them in programs that open their eyes, minds and hearts to the needs in our community and world, and teach them that they can make a difference as they use their gifts.

Our school relies on the dedication and sacrifices of our parents. Our school is one of the most important ministries of our parish. It evangelizes our students and their families and gives witness to the essence of the Catholic way of life.

Our faculty and staff are LAY MINISTERS! They live and share their faith. They love our children, they love learning, and they love teaching.

Years ago, a boy in an Indiana farm town graduated from the eight grade. His father gave him a two dollar bill and a small card with seven points to live by. The boy, John Wooden, grew up to be a great basketball coach and always honored the points on the card.

1) Be true to yourself

2) Help others

3) Make each day your masterpiece

4) Drink deeply from good books

5) Make friendship a fine art

6) Build shelter against a rainy day

7) Pray for guidance and give thanks for your blessings each day

I am proud that our school and our faculty teach these seven points! ♛

This week the school year begins. We are excited along with the children and parents as they enter the rhythm of the school days, the adventures of learning, and the joy of being with their friends and making new friends.

Our parish grade school is poised for a great year. Our faculty and administration are rested and prepared to share their wisdom, joy and faith with our children. Summer vacation for them is not only a time of rest, but also a time to make preparations to go even deeper into their ministry as teachers. The school and classrooms are spruced up and we are ready to go. Even more so, the entire school community is ready to dive in.

Our students have had the summer to rest, to grow, to evaluate any changes they need to make, and to savor and trust the growth that has taken place in each of their lives. One of the great gifts that students can give one another as they move from year to year is that they encourage one another to honor the development and changes. That is one of the mysteries of life...we are who we are in grade school...and even as growth, learning and development certainly occur...to a great extent, we remain who we are...and yet we become who we are meant to be. I think that is why many people who were friends in grade school and high school stay friends throughout their lives...they have "grown up together."

Our Catholic School and Lexington Catholic High School exist in order to give every student a foundation in the way of Jesus and the teachings and spirit of the Catholic Church. We are seeking to prepare our youth to be strong Catholic leaders. Through Religion classes, regular Mass attendance, prayer in the classroom, sacramental preparation and sacramental deepening, and through projects of Christian service, our students are taught to live their faith.

Wednesday is the first day of the school year. As we move into the school year, the *Feast of the Assumption of Mary* is celebrated this Tuesday, the day before the school year begins. It is a Holy Day as we commemorate how at the end of her life Mary was taken into heaven. I encourage you to offer special prayers on this feast day.

> *Let us ask Mary to inspire us all to seek and respond to the Gifts of the Holy Spirit and to live as people of wisdom, compassion, joy and prayerful peace.*

Let us ask Mary, the mother of Jesus and our mother to watch over our children and to bless them with her prayers for their success and joy this year.

Let us ask Mary, who taught Jesus, to be a source of wisdom for all teachers, aides, and parents as they all seek to guide our children.

Let us ask Mary, who saw and experienced that nothing is impossible with God, to help us all to be faithful in our prayers if and when difficult situations occur in the midst of the school year.

Let us ask Mary to inspire us all to seek and respond to the Gifts of the Holy Spirit and to live as people of wisdom, compassion, joy and prayerful peace. ♛

# CHAPTER 5

*Christian Unity:*

BULLETIN — January 26, 2020

Today with our 11:30 a.m. Mass we begin our observance of Catholic Schools' Week. Later this week, on Wednesday, we will host the Diocesan "Mega Mass" with schools from throughout the diocese being represented by their students. Catholic schools have the mission of forming students to live as followers of Jesus who base their lives on Catholic teachings and the Catholic way of life. Many of the leaders in our community have developed their gifts and formed their ideals and principles through their education in Catholic Schools. We are particularly proud of our own parish school, a two-time Blue Ribbon School. We give thanks today in a special way for all the members of our school's faculty and staff, the members of our school council and our P.T.O. as they give of themselves with a spirit of ministry.

I share the gratitude of our entire community for our Diocesan Catholic Education Opportunities Foundation which is being launched this February. We congratulate Kim Thompson, from our parish and school, who has been named the Executive Director. And I offer thanks to the members of our parish who have been part of the development of this foundation whose purpose is to generate scholarship money so that more youth will be able to receive their education in our Catholic schools.

Even as we celebrate Catholic Schools, we also celebrate today the dedication and ingenuity of our families as they take responsibility for their children's faith formation through CCD, Home Schooling, and groups like the American Heritage Girls. Today is the day of the American Heritage Girls' Chili Cook-Off. I trust that for some of our parishioners, this event will be the highlight of the weekend. Once again, I am honored to serve as one of the judges.

A vibrant life is full of "both-ands". I appreciate our school and our faculty and staff; I appreciate private, public and other schools which operate on Christian principles, and whose faculty and staff live and share their faith in ways that inspire the students. (In many of our diocesan counties, there is no Catholic school, and yet Catholic faculty and staff live their faith and serve as evangelizers.) To live in the "both-and" world does not preclude priorities...that's why we have a school and why we invest so much in it.

"Both-and." Children need a good faith formation in their schools and religion classes — but even more so, they need the example and encouragement of their parents. Schools and CCD programs are both important — but the fidelity of parents to their ministry of passing on the faith is paramount.

One more example of the "both-and-ness" of life is relevant today. This Sunday at 7 p.m. there will be a prayer service at Pax Christi Church as the culmination of Christian Unity Week. We are grateful for the ministry of every Christian denomination and of every Christian congregation.

Our Church sense has developed in such a way that many of us are appreciative when a family member or friend, coming from a background of Catholicism, and having shifted into a life devoid of religious practice or involvement, then makes a decision and starts going to church again — but it is not a Catholic Church. We are glad that our loved one is living with faith and seeking to know and follow Jesus. And yet, we believe that there is a best way...and that is why we love our Catholic faith. It is not always easy to balance the two...but we can be both ecumenical and Catholic. ♛

# CHAPTER 6

*Valentine's Day:*

BULLETIN — February 12, 2017

BULLETIN — February 14, 2021

This Tuesday we celebrate the feast of St. Valentine. On Valentine's Day it is customary to give flowers, candy or cards and notes expressing affection to those we love. Valentine's Day is a special opportunity to highlight the importance of the written word. Valentine's Day is one of the largest sale days when cards and love notes are sent and received.

One of the joys of being a priest here at a parish with a school is that I occasionally am deluged with appreciation notes from the students in school. Often students write a series of notes and cards to the residents of nursing homes. In the Sacrament of reconciliation, I have sometimes given a penance to children to "write an I love you note" to one of their older family members.

Writing is important. Whether professional or writing in leisure time, many people who write do so every day. Once they start writing, they may not be sure where it will go, but they trust the process. Many people have developed special friendships with pen pals. Soldiers, students away at college and prisoners always appreciate mail. Very often the biography of famous person is supplemented by their correspondence. Some romances and wonderful marriages refer back to exchanged letters as a key to moving to a next level of intimacy. One of my priest classmates saves every Christmas card and letter, and in the course of a year, reads one a day and prays for the sender. Even people who do not feel that they have the gift of writing will often spend an inordinate amount of time shopping for the card that expresses just what they want to say.

It is always an honor to write a letter of recommendation for someone I know who is seeking to advance in their job or in their academic career. Many people pray best by the use of a prayer journal, at least for a season of their lives. It is helpful to many people's prayer lives to honestly say on paper what we desire to say to God, and then to simply take some time to listen.

Saint Valentine
PATRON SAINT OF LOVE

When something difficult needs to be said to a friend, co-worker, or someone for whom we have responsibility, it is helpful to write out (and rehearse) what we want to say, and how we want to say it...then to envision two different kinds of responses from the person challenged, and then to write out our next response. These kinds of encounters are never perfect; but there are some ways to control the chaos.

St. Paul wrote Epistles as educational love letters to communities of early Christians. The writings of Pope Francis are guiding our Church to be a Church of Mercy. In preparing homilies, many ministers write the homily out, and count on the Holy Spirit to give them the right words while composing, and also to give them the right words when delivering.

In this era of texting and tweeting, the art of writing is in danger of being de-emphasized. We do well to honor the fast and the efficient ways of communication, but also to preserve traditional writing with its aspects of reflectiveness and more thorough expressiveness. ♛

This weekend we celebrate St. Valentine's Day, a day for sending cards, giving gifts, and expressing love and affection. We live in an era of ever-increasing ease and speed in sending written messages. Sometimes these messages are regretted; they are sent too quickly, without the necessary thought and reflection. Valentine's Day serves as an opportunity to review some of the more noble aspects of writing.

Many people journal as a way of processing life, expressing and understanding themselves, and often as a basis for prayer. Journals are like diaries: private and for the eyes of the writer and the eyes of God.

Thank you notes make a big difference in life. Thank you notes are a gift in return and often help the sender to become more generous.

Many of us make our list: grocery lists, phone call lists, job lists...very often when people examine their consciences before going to confession, they make a list of what they need to mention. Very often we plan the day by means of a list and refer to it through the day.

Sometimes writing helps us to analyze and understand some of the painful and awkward situations of life. Occasionally we write a kind of rehearsal of a difficult conversation that needs to take place, a conversation of confrontation, apology, or forgiveness.

Writing helps us to organize our thoughts and clarify what we feel needs to be said. Many preachers, including me, write our Sunday sermons in order to speak as clearly and as helpfully as we can. Let us give thanks for poets, song writers, spiritual writers, and even down-home muses.

Writing is very helpful when we feel there has been a misunderstanding. Writing clarifies what we desire to communicate and it is an invitation for another to do the same.

Writing is a means of teaching, giving directions, sharing history, telling the news. What is written often provides a path as we navigate uncharted territory in our journey of life. Writing frees us to tell our story and to enter into the cosmic story.

On this day we focus on the words on the Valentine Cards...words penned by another and yet chosen as a gift to give. We also realize that many of us write our own message on the cards we send as we express affection...and love and even romance!

Many of us have been doing more reading than usual during the pandemic. We appreciate good writing. We appreciate authors who make our life journeys clearer and better. An author who writes with authority uses that power to touch our hearts in a positive manner. The Ultimate Author who blesses us is Our God. God's Word has changed so many lives, been the foundation for so much virtue, and the Word of God became flesh!

This day let us all deepen our commitment to write in a way that enhances our lives and the lives of others. Whether with pen or at keyboard or on a mobile device...let us open our minds and souls to what God is writing in and through us. ♛

# CHAPTER 7

## *Ordinary Time and a New Ordinary:*

BULLETIN — January 12, 2020

BULLETIN — May 31, 2020

The *Feast of the Baptism of Jesus* is the culmination of the Christmas season. It is the Church's observance of Jesus entering into his ministry. Jesus leaves behind his family and his home and begins his ministry of preaching, teaching, healing, and developing evangelizers. He makes the shift into the ordinary but extra-ordinary ministry of day by day activities which will provide salvation for the world.

From the standpoint of the Church year, this Monday we return to Ordinary time. Generally the priests and deacons will wear green vestments at Mass in the Ordinary Time. Ordinary time does not mean "low level time". Rather it is the time when our ordinary days are ordered by the spirit and the joy and the dynamism of the preceding season...in effect, we are now called to live in the spirit of Jesus born once again in our hearts. Ordinary living and standard procedure for a Christian is to live with great faith, hope and love...it is to live in harmony with our Baptismal promises.

We promise at Baptism to reject sin and the temptations that lead us to sin; we pledge to live the faith we profess in the Creed; we count on family and godparents to encourage us by word and deed; and we serve as godparents and village-mentors for one another as we seek to live as followers of Jesus.

The Advent season has alerted us to the plight of the poor in our community and the difference we can make by our compassion and generosity. Unfortunately, there is some ordinariness to their needs. Hopefully, our compassion and generosity will be an ordinary part of our lives throughout the year.

Christmas has been a time of increased Mass attendance, extra prayers and humble reflections on God's goodness and our own need for God's grace. Now in the ordinary time of the year, it will be wonderful if such heightened prayerfulness and spirituality become standard procedure.

Christmas and the end of the year are occasions when many of us respond generously to the needs of our parish and special collections. However, we have our ordinary expenses here at the parish and throughout the diocese. We encourage you to have an ordinary and steady approach to financial stewardship; to regularly budget your gift to assist in the parish's ministry.

The Diocesan Annual Appeal responds to the needs of the Church's ministry all throughout our mission diocese. I hope and pray that a part of the ordinary orientation of our minds and hearts is to the needs of the Church in Eastern Kentucky and ministering to refugees and immigrants. Our response to the Diocesan Annual Appeal is in need of a boost. Next weekend, Deacon Bill Grimes, who founded and directs the New Hope Clinic in Owingsville, in Bath county, will preach at all our Masses about the needs of Eastern Kentucky and how our response to the Diocesan Appeal makes a difference in these areas of such great need.

So we move forward...we move into ordinary time. We are an extra-ordinary cathedral, made up of ordinary people who rise to extra-ordinary heights time and time again as we open ourselves to God's grace — which is beyond the extra-ordinary. ♛

This Sunday is the *Feast of Pentecost*, when the Holy Spirit came upon the disciples and empowered them to live and to share the Good News about Jesus. Pentecost is called the birthday of the Church. In many ways, Pentecost this year is a day of rebirth for Christ the King parish.

We will reopen our beautiful cathedral church for Sunday Masses this weekend. We look forward to being with fellow parishioners and being able to receive Jesus in Holy Communion. This return to Mass together is one more sign that our world and our local community are making progress as we seek to diminish the power of the pandemic.

Yet, the pandemic is not over — nor is the caution we need to take. Our re-opening will be a slow and gradual process. Our gathering this weekend for Mass will not be like the way we have been gathering in church for years. We need to wear masks. We need to be socially distanced from one another. Our church with a capacity of almost 1000 will be able to seat around 100 people. You will need to enter and exit at the glass doors leading into Hehman Hall. A team of ushers will be seating you. You need to depart as Mass ends. There will be no physical contact during the Lord's Prayer or the Sign of Peace. Holy Communion will only offered as the consecrated host and received only in the hand. There will be restrictions implemented in order to keep you and everyone else safe. Like you, I wish we could all be as normal as we were in early March; but we need to be safe and cautious.

We will be using an online ticketing system, *Eventbrite*. And so, everyone coming to worship will need a ticket. An usher will take your ticket; another usher will seat you. At least for the summer, we will have an added Mass, at 2:30 p.m. on Sunday afternoon; our 9 a.m. Mass on Sunday has been moved to 9:30 a.m. Therefore, our weekend schedule is 5 p.m. on Saturday and on Sunday, 7:30 a.m., 9:30 a.m., 11:30 a.m., 2:30 p.m. and 5 p.m.

We realize that there is the possibility that not everyone who desires to come to Sunday Mass will be able to get a ticket; we are planning to make adjustments as we go along in order to give every parishioner an equal opportunity.

At the present time, we are still working on plans for our daily Mass schedule and scheduled confessions. We are continuing with the practice of hearing confessions by appointment. And we encourage you to continue attending virtual Masses.

Please keep in mind that our pope and our bishop have dispensed us from our obligation to attend Sunday Mass. Many of you will make a better and healthier choice to stay at home and pray while attending a virtual Mass.

What we will be doing is far from ideal; but it is bringing us back into church, back to praying together as a community of faith...even though masked, socially distant, with less singing and with less freedom of space than we are accustomed to at church.

We have a very skilled and dedicated ad-hoc committee helping us work out our plans for re-opening. I am grateful to them. However, I do add that we are in need of more volunteers to serve as ushers and to help sanitize the church following each Mass.

We need your cooperation as we reopen so that we can do so in a way that is safe and prayerful. I thank you in advance as we take this first step of reopening, as we seek to praise God, and as we humbly pray for the gifts of God's Holy Spirit as we rebuild physically, emotionally, economically and spiritually. Let us pray together that we as a community of faith will take this first step as well as we can and let us pray for the safety and healing of our brothers and sisters throughout the world. ♛

# CHAPTER 8

*St. Joseph:*

BULLETIN — January 3, 2021

A
s we begin the new year, Pope Francis has called for the people of the Church to trust St. Joseph as our patron throughout the year. Just as Francis guided us to count on Mary's intercession during the dreadful and deadly year 2020, now as we foresee the eradication of the pandemic, we count on Joseph to guide us by his prayers and example of prudence and patience.

Joseph is a model of responsibility. He was the foster-father of Jesus. He realized that God was the Father of Jesus. He knew his place. He respected the virginity of Mary, even as he deeply cherished her and they had an intimate love. So, he is an example for all of us of restraint, respect, humility and purity. He was less concerned with his role within the Holy Family, and more concerned with giving.

Joseph is the patron of workers. He is regarded as a carpenter, or perhaps a person who worked with stone. It is a common image to portray Joseph teaching young Jesus to work with his hands. Luke's Gospel tells us that "Jesus grew in wisdom and knowledge". Joseph was certainly a teacher and a mentor for the growing Jesus.

The Gospels describe Joseph and Mary as betrothed at the time when Mary conceived Jesus by the Holy Spirit. "Betrothed" means engaged and united, but the wedding ceremony has not yet taken place and the couple is not living together. Joseph knows that he is not the father of this child and he is prepared to do what it takes to preserve Mary's dignity and reputation. Soon after his birth, Joseph and Mary present Jesus in the temple as they dedicate him to God; later

*Photo by Maureen Guarnieri-Yeager*

they face the loss of Jesus at the time of a temple visit and, upon finding him, Joseph hears those poignant words of Jesus, "I must be about my Father's work."

Today, on this feast of the Epiphany, our imaginations can easily write the script of Joseph's conversations with the Magi coming to give gifts and homage to his infant son and the attendant reflection with Mary about the meaning of their visit.

Joseph of the Holy Family has some parallels with the First Testament Joseph. Both Josephs heard the Word of God in their dreams. Joseph took the Holy Family to Egypt and back in order to keep them safe; Joseph in the Book of Genesis brings his father and siblings to Egypt so that they can be saved from the famine in Palestine. Both Josephs were men of mercy. One of the most powerful passage in Genesis is when Joseph reveals his identity to his brothers who had beat him up and left him for dead. "I am your brother, Joseph," he said through his tears. Joseph, betrothed to Mary, not understanding the mystery of her pregnancy, "sought to divorce her quietly."

As we enter into 2021, Joseph is a great model...may we do our work with joy and efficiency (and may there be enough work for all)...Let us trust our God-given dreams to clarify our mission in life. May we live as people of mercy. May we trust that a pure life is the way to joy. And may Joseph guide us as we make the journey from the state of the pandemic to a new land of freedom and normalcy. ♛

# CHAPTER 9

*Loving Our Kiddos:*

BULLETIN — April 22, 2018

BULLETIN — July 8, 2018

This week our school's eighth grade class will be on their trip to Washington, D.C. This is an educational trip, and a time for joy and deepening of friendships. In a way it is one more aspect of the passage from grade school to high school. But there will also be some element of a PILGRIMAGE on such a trip. It is an opportunity to feel the spirit of our nation, to understand the history and the great acts of courage, integrity, faith and vision which have shaped our nation, and to be affected by the qualities of great leaders and ordinary people doing the extraordinary. We are grateful for the ministry of Karie Boneau and Andrew Dombrowski as they guide this trip, but also very appreciative of all who go as chaperones and fellow pilgrims. We are very glad that Fr. Kiran will be on this trip as chaplain and as one more pilgrim, as he has his first experience of Washington, D. C.

This is also the week leading into First Communion for the children of our parish. It is a week of special prayer and preparation, practices, confessions and retreats. Many of our families are also making special preparations for family members coming in from out of town and for the gathering of friends at a party. First Communion in a way is also a rite of passage...now the children have learned enough to appreciate Jesus coming into their lives. The children who have been yearning — hungering — to go to Holy Communion are now able to do so.

It is the beginning of an uncountable number of Holy Communions which will take place in their lives over the upcoming years. They, like us, will receive Jesus at times when they are very grateful for life's blessings, but also in times of fear, weakness, confusion, doubt and self-doubt. And the bottom line is that Jesus will always be ready to come into their hearts and give them the gifts they need.

Next Saturday at the 5 p.m. Mass, our CCD children will make their First Holy Communions; next Sunday at a 2 p.m. Mass, the grade school children will be making their First Holy Communions. They and their families, and all of us invite you to join us at either or both Masses. I thank all parents and catechists who have guided the children on their PILGRIMAGE to this great day, a day that they will remember all their lives.

Keep in mind also that the next day, Monday, April 30 is Grandparents' Day at our school. That is a special day to celebrate the powerful love of grandparents and to be grateful for the blessings they bring to their adult children and their grandkids, as crucial members of the "village" raising our children. In a unique way, grandparents can share the lessons they have learned on their PILGRIMAGES through life and serve as guides and cheerleaders for the next generation of pilgrims. ♛

*Photo by Maureen Guarnieri-Yeager*

When I was first ordained as a priest, my first assignment was at Holy Family Church in Ashland as an assistant pastor and high school teacher. One of my favorite memories goes back to the time of leading a team of parishioners to develop the parish's first Vacation Bible School. A sister from the Diocesan Office of Education helped us choose our curriculum and helped our volunteer faculty to be prepared for our five morning sessions. Our faculty consisted of parishioners who were mothers, but one man who worked at Ashland Oil took a week of vacation to teach with us and a man who worked the night shift at Armco Steel also taught. Some of the high school students were also volunteers. We had a piano player and a song leader, and I served as the beginning and ending emcee. Several of the men in the parish teamed up to build elaborate sets in the classrooms and in the gym. The coordinator of the Bible School was "Bible School Betty". Many of the kids who came for the week of Bible School brought friends from their neighborhood, and so there was a kind of ecumenical aspect to our Bible School.

A few years ago, I drove the aging Fr. Wil Fraenzle through the area of his beloved parish and missions in Lee and Owsley Counties. In Heidelberg, near Contrary Creek, we stopped at a country store for a soft drink and the lady who waited on us reminisced about the neighborhood Bible School held at St. Therese Church's. She spoke about how much she enjoyed attending the Catholics' Bible School every summer while growing up.

During the week of July 23 our annual Bible School will take place, every evening from 5:30 p.m. till 8:30 p.m. It will have the theme of the Vatican Express. We are grateful and amazed at the work that Karen Kirkland does in organizing and guiding the Bible School. We are grateful for all who will be giving of themselves in many different ways to make it a memorable experience for the children and their families.

Recently I saw the movie, *Won't You Be My Neighbor?*, about Mr. Rogers. He was dedicated to treating small children with love and respect and teaching them important lessons at an early age. A Vacation Bible School does not have the ability to teach any lofty theological concepts, but always has a way of conveying that life is good, that God loves us all, that we are all brothers and sisters, that the Church is a friendly and joyful place, and that God and good people love us as we are. The kids learn songs which they sing all week and beyond, they have lots of fun and have some great snacks, they make new friends, they do learn some important and fundamental lessons, and they spread their joy throughout their families.

We are a cathedral and a village. We highlighted our cathedral nature as we hosted the powerful Ecumenical Prayer Service in mid-June for people from churches throughout the city as we prayed for the families separated at our Southern border. And with our Vacation Bible School, we will express our village nature as we care for and delight in the children of our community. ♛

# CHAPTER 10

## *Lent:*

BULLETIN — February 25, 2018

BULLETIN — March 3, 2019

O ne of the devotions particularly linked to the Lenten season is the meditation entitled the Stations of the Cross. Drawing from scripture and from other reflections on Good Friday, the Stations recreate the walk of Jesus through the streets of Jerusalem as he carried his cross to Calvary.

The origin of the Way of the Cross is grounded in the desire of Christians on the early centuries to make a pilgrimage to Jerusalem and to prayerfully walk on the same ground that Jesus walked on as he struggled to Calvary. As it was realized that making a pilgrimage was not possible for many people, the path was re-created in many outdoor settings in the vicinity of churches. A set of 14 meditations developed. They were based on stations or "stopping points" as Jesus ministered or experienced particular sufferings while he was making his way to the hill of his crucifixion. Eventually plaques or painting of the stations of the cross were erected as works of art on the interior walls of churches, and people would walk individually or as a group from station to station, praying and meditating as they walked.

During the season of Lent, we have a community prayer of the Stations of the Cross every Friday following the 5:30 p.m. Mass. As we pray the Way of the Cross, we are moved to pity Jesus, but also to admire his faith. Yet the deeper result is that this devotion leads us to follow Jesus.

As we pray the Stations of the Cross, our reflections can go in many different directions. We are moved by the great love of Jesus for humanity, for you and me, a love so great that he gave his life for us and endured such suffering on Good Friday. We are inspired to have compassion for the people we know who are suffering. We realize that Jesus felt the pain of betrayal, denial, callousness, and being used as a pawn in religious-political conflicts. We see the cruelty and disregard of Pilate, the soldiers, and the crowd. We feel the intensity of Veronica, the women of Jerusalem, the beloved disciple, and especially Mary, his mother. We often accompany our meditations with the song "Stabat Mater", "at the cross her station keeping", and we walk with Mary as she supports Jesus and grieves over her son's horrific ordeal. We share the ambivalence of Simon of Cyrene, called upon to help carry the cross of a man he had never before encountered.

We encounter Jesus as we pray the stations, and we are reminded that even as we suffer, even as we experience life's unfairness, we can still be givers, we can still minister, we can still make a difference by our prayers, by our concern for others, by our trust in God, by our patience. The stations of the cross provide a reflection on one of the prime paradoxes of life...when we are powerless, we still have the power to give; when we are victimized, we still can make a difference by our courage and compassion for others; when we are saddened by someone else's suffering, that sadness can move us not only to offer consolation but also to do what we can to change a culture that only tolerates and encourages injustice and violence.

The Stations of the Cross take us back into Salvation History, 2000 years ago, but they speak to us today. It makes sense that a prime Good Friday hymn is "Were you there", and the answer is yes because Jesus continues to call us to follow him and to minister to contemporary brothers and sisters who carry their cross. ♔

Lent is a time of conversion. Conversion does not just mean that a person who is not Catholic becomes Catholic; the more basic meaning of conversion is a change of one's life for the better. Conversion can happen in several areas of our lives...spiritual, intellectual, moral, relational, emotional, and physical. It is not a good idea to try to focus on all these areas during one six week period of Lent. Prayerful discernment helps us to know what we need to commit ourselves to in this Lenten season. As a means of assistance, I will address these six aspects of conversion and some possible Lenten practices in each of these areas.

Spiritual conversion can mean a deeper and more regular practice of prayer, a stronger commitment to the Church, or a more real friendship with Jesus. The means to such growth may include blocking out a daily prayer time, weekday Mass attendance, praying the rosary or stations, making a retreat or mission, Eucharistic Adoration, or reading and praying with the Bible.

Intellectual conversion can mean a focused study of the Sacraments, or the nature of the Church, or how current difficult situations have parallels in Church history. Intellectual conversion involves good reading, attending a lecture, participating in a faith-sharing group, or reading biographies and especially having an open mind to learn the unexpected. Many advocates for justice have undergone a profound intellectual conversion — they see how unjust practices are connected and can be eradicated.

Moral conversion means to change our actions and attitudes which miss the mark of how we know God wants us to live and how we know others need us to live. Moral conversion is often related to a practice of self-discipline, but also means cultivating virtues such as compassion, generosity, and integrity. The quest for moral conversion often involves fasting from food, drink, or some of the pleasures, diversions, conversations and thoughts that take us to a slippery moral slope. Moral conversion involves saying no to some things, but even more importantly, saying yes to what is right and good. The Sacrament of Reconciliation helps many of us to morally convert.

Relational conversion often means forgiveness or opening a heart that has been closed to another. It is not uncommon for there to be alienation and resentments in families or for friendships to be lost. Specific petitionary prayer is a good Lenten practice in such cases, seeking a mutually best time to talk, perhaps doing some letter writing, journaling, or compassionate analysis of what happened and why. Relational conversion also means seeking to listen more, to be more of a friend, performing charitable works, and more frequently expressing appreciation and encouragement.

Emotional conversion refers to moving from inner chaos to inner peace, from reactivity to proactivity, from rage to passion, from regret about the past and fear of the future to grateful acceptance of the here and now. Emotional conversion involves making time for contemplation, walking in the woods, doing a hobby, listening to good music, savoring art, a good meal with friends and family, cooking, yard work, even naps (During Lent? why not? Lent is about growth!) For some of us, emotional conversion involves counseling, spiritual direction or confession that addresses the attitudes at the heart of inner turmoil.

Physical conversion means becoming more healthy. It is not simply our program to look good for the summer. It involves exercise, healthy eating and drinking, getting enough rest, and keeping work in perspective. It is best to start moderately and to build up. The ideal reason is to have enough energy to be the disciple that the Lord is calling us to be. It is helpful to have a coach, to have an accountability system, and to have supportive friends.

I offer these six areas as suggestions and prompters for you to prayerfully reflect on how Jesus is calling you to the next step of the never-ending process of conversion. May the Holy Spirit bless us all with a fruitful and holy Lenten season! ◼

# CHAPTER 11

*Holy Week and Easter:*

BULLETIN — March 27, 2016

BULLETIN — April 1, 2018

BULLETIN — April 12, 2020

BULLETIN — April 4, 2021

Throughout Lent, many of us read and prayed with our parish Christmas gift, *Rediscover Jesus*. Written by the noted Catholic evangelist, Matthew Kelly, *Rediscover Jesus* maintains that as we come to know Jesus we are able to deal with the ultimate questions of life, such as who am I?...who is God?...what matters most and least?...what will my contribution be?...what happens when we die? Matthew Kelly further suggests that the time for a new beginning is NOW and that we will find the answers to the deepest questions in life through our relationship with Jesus.

Easter is the ultimate moment of rediscovering Jesus. Jesus the rabbi, preacher, healer and leader was perceived in an entirely different manner upon his rising from the dead. Easter and our personal experience of the Risen Jesus changes our lives and blesses us with light as we face the problems, questions and mysteries of life.

Through this Holy Week, our special liturgies and prayers set the stage for our Easter Alleluias. Palm Sunday ushers in the week as we recall the adulation for Christ the Messiah and then his rejection by the chosen people who did not understand his message or accept his method

> *The Easter Vigil begins our celebration of the Resurrection. We rejoice with Christ, the Light of the world. We light our Easter candle, bless our Easter water, and celebrate Baptism, Confirmation, and First Communion with the new members of our Church.*

of redemption. Holy Thursday presents the Last Supper, with its institution of the Eucharist as Jesus empowered his apostles and their successors to transform the bread and wine into his Body and Blood. On Good Friday we are edified by the courage and integrity of Jesus as he suffers and continues to minister until he dies. In a very real sense, we walk with Jesus to Calvary, we pray with and for him, and we feel the grief of Mary and the confusion of his disciples. On Holy Saturday, we quietly ponder the possibility of a world without Jesus. We face our own fears and doubts as we yearn for the light that Jesus can bring.

The Easter Vigil begins our celebration of the Resurrection. We rejoice with Christ, the Light of the world. We light our Easter candle, bless our Easter water, and celebrate Baptism, Confirmation, and First Communion with the new members of our Church. We review the history of salvation and people's hope for a Messiah who would liberate the world from its darkness. As Jesus emerges from the tomb, as we meditate on the post-resurrection appearances of Jesus, and even as we visualize his empty tomb...we rediscover Jesus, and we take a major step towards discovering our true selves and the meaning of our lives. ♛

As an amateur photographer, I have often enjoyed taking and the savoring a picture of a beautiful sunrise, with the range of colors with which God blesses our sky. Sunrises are beautiful, but they also offer the gift of hope as a new day dawns. In 1982 I was on a pilgrimage in the Holy Land. Our group hiked to the top of Mount Sinai and as the day was dawning and the sun was rising, we had Mass at the location where God gave the 10 Commandments to Moses. On occasion I have started my Easter morning by attending a Sunrise Service at the Lexington Cemetery. In the midst of the natural beauty of its grounds, the history, the grave sites, and the multitude of tears and memories which are part of the cemetery environment, I know that many people have come to cemeteries and prayed and asked for the prayers of and have sought to draw wisdom and hope from the spirits of their deceased friends and family members.

Easter and the resurrection of Jesus remind us of the reality of hope. The darkness of death is not everlasting but is the beginning of new life. The Easter Candle symbolizes the light of Christ burning in the darkness. Sometimes the Easter Vigil is celebrated as an all-night vigil, beginning in the darkness and concluding at sunrise. We need not say that Jesus literally rose from the dead at dawn; but we believe that his resurrection brought light to a world darkened by the apparent victory of sin and the attendant sense of futility and nihilism. At the Easter Vigil liturgy, we begin in the dark of night, we proclaim Christ is our Light, our candles speak of the power of the light of Christ in us, we sing in an exultant way of the Easter Candle and the light of Jesus, and the first reading speaks of creation...where a dark chaos covered the earth, and God's Spirit breathed, and there was LIGHT...and it was good. The Gospel of John, which we will read frequently in this upcoming season, has a prominent theme of the power of the forces of darkness and how the power of Jesus the light of the world will always prevail over the darkness.

The Resurrection of Jesus promises eternal life for all of us. It is the crowning moment of the mystery of the way that Jesus redeems us and gives us new life. The resurrection guides us to freedom...freedom from fear, freedom from sin, freedom from addictions, freedom from compulsions, freedom from doubt, freedom from self-destruction, freedom from gloom.

Christmas and Easter are regarded as highlights of the year for every Christian. They both focus on the great love of Jesus, and of God entering and sanctifying humanity. Christmas and Easter are major breakthroughs as the mystery of God's desire for us continues to unfold. It is no wonder that a common scripture passage for both seasons is "The people who walked in darkness have seen a great light." (Isaiah 9:1)

My prayer for you is that you feel the great love of Jesus for you, your family, and for all the people of our world during this Easter Sunday and throughout your life. Let us walk together as people of the LIGHT! ◼

I am confident that there are many commentaries this year on the uniqueness of this year's celebration of Easter. It will be a celebration without people coming to Church, with an entirely different approach to the Easter parade, Easter egg hunts and Easter dinner. But that does not mean that this will not be an Easter of great prayer, family love and encouragement to one another.

Restraint continues to be a key theme. Restraint and patience are at the heart of our approach to protecting ourselves, our loved ones and our world during this time of the pandemic. It is striking that the Easter Gospels focus more on the empty tomb than on the exhilarating and clarifying experience of encounters with the Resurrected Jesus. The disciples needed to be patient, to trust that the day of the powerful and close personal encounters with Jesus would eventually come. So too, we need to stay with our strategy of social distancing. We are not at the end of our ordeal. Our days of close encounters with Jesus in the physical reception of Holy Communion and our close encounters with

friends, co-workers and neighbors, and co-worshippers will come. But they are not here yet. We need restraint and patience.

Easter's Gospel passage presents the Beloved Disciple, an unnamed figure who represents all of us, even if we do not recognize God's love for us. He goes to the tomb with St. Peter; the Beloved Disciple arrives first, but out of deference, he restrains himself from entering first. When he enters, he is able to see the rumpled linens in the tomb with the eyes of faith. He trusts the power of Mary Magdalene to be an effective messenger of the Good News. Like the Beloved Disciple, let us also be people of restraint as we wait our time, as we seek to see with the eyes of faith, and as we trust and honor the ministry of those who are serving in the trenches.

This Easter is also a day that presents the challenge and opportunity to concentrate on the specialness of every Easter. First of all, realizing we can spend Easter in our pajamas or shorts and a T-shirt, let's make sure we dress up, even if we live alone, even if no one sees us. Second, let's find a way to rejoice in the beauties of spring. Let's also find a special way to reach out to at least one more person beyond our household, beyond our family, with a card, a call, or a prayer. And beyond attending Mass via livestream, let's find one more way to bring prayer into the day.

Lent has reminded us that we need Jesus, that he is with us, that he weeps with us, heals us, and he guides us to live in new and renewed ways. Resurrection reminds us that Jesus is with us and that we are called to new life as a community. Just as Peter, Mary Magdalen and the Beloved Disciple did not function alone and brought different personal gifts to the proclamation of the Good News of that First Easter, so too, we are part of a community which can work together to flatten the curve, to live with restraint, and to prepare ourselves and our world for that day when we can all emerge from the cocoons of our sheltered places.

Trust the alleluias...sing the alleluias as best you can...live the alleluias!!! ▥

I offer strong sentiments of gratitude for all who have helped our Church to pray at our Masses and other services during this Holy Week. Last year we were only able to livestream the services. This year we were able to advance to a limited number of people who could be physically present. Hopefully, next year's Holy Week and this year's Christmas will be occasions when we can fill our cathedral.

There are many people and groups for which I am very grateful...our ushers, our deacons, our music ministers, cantors, mini-choirs, lectors, and all who worked to make our sanctuary beautifully convey the moods of each day, and all those who helped us to work out our plans to seat people in Church, in Hehman Hall and to provide Holy Communion for those who could only attend Mass in their vehicles.

I give thanks also for all who have been members of the committee guiding the renovation of Hehman Hall. The new look is very beautiful and inviting and will enhance our commitment to be a place of hospitality and community events. Our many projects sponsored by the blessings of our Capital Campaign continue and we are putting our parish in place for the next chapters of our life as a community of faith.

We are all grateful that spring has been marked by a decrease in the threats from the Corona virus. However, the battle against the pandemic is not yet over. We still need to follow a safety protocol to keep everyone safe. We encourage all to get the vaccines and thereby keep ourselves and others safe.

I continue to be amazed and heartened by the creative ways our parish and school have made adaptations so that our ministries can keep touching peoples' lives in helpful ways. I am grateful for the continual financial support which you are giving to our church and our parish ministries and the ways you are generously responding to the needs of the poor.

The core of this Easter and every Easter is Jesus. Jesus has risen from the dead. The forces and powers that sought to erase him and render Jesus irrelevant are not the final word. In the Gracious Mystery of God, Jesus rises from the dead; during the Easter season we will celebrate the appearances of the Risen Jesus to his disciples; he will shine as the Light of the world and he will prepare his disciples to receive and to implement the Gifts of the Holy Spirit which will empower them to begin the Church.

The Risen Jesus is a glorious beacon of hope. In our world so stricken by the pandemic, the Resurrection reminds us that death and illness will not prevail and that better days are ahead. In a world with so much civil discord, prejudice and injustice, economic instability, and so many temptations to live in a self-centered and acidic manner, the Light of Jesus guides us through the darkness. And so we sing in the best way that our masks will permit us..."Alleluia, Alleluia, Alleluia." ♛

# CHAPTER 12

## *AA at Christ the King:*

BULLETIN — February 3, 2019

This week, on Monday evening at 7 p.m. at St. Elizabeth Ann Seton Church, Bishop John Stowe, OFM Conv., will celebrate a *Mass of Remembrance and Healing* for those who lives have been impacted by drug addiction. The Mass is for those who have died from their use of drugs, those who are struggling with addictions, and for their loved ones. At 5:30 p.m., there will be confessions available at St. Elizabeth Ann Seton.

I encourage you to come, and even if you "do not qualify", to come and to offer prayerful support. The availability and the use of illegal drugs is a terrible problem throughout our nation and also in our community. Many of us have family members or friends who are affected by drug addiction.

I am honored that our parish hosts both Alcoholics Anonymous groups, and also Al-Anon, which is for the family members of those struggling with an alcohol addiction. Family members face a special challenge as they try to find the right mix of tough love, fidelity, forgiveness and the avoidance of enabling. The AA approach has spawned groups for those addicted to drugs, sex, gambling and other areas of self-destruction.

The Franciscan evangelist, Father Richard Rohr, maintains that the most unique contribution from the U.S.A. to the spirituality of people throughout the world has been the 12-step approach of AA. Spiritual directors and authors have employed the 12-step approach in helping people pray better, work through compulsiveness, and come to live more balanced lives.

The twelves steps begin with the humble (and humbled) admission of a problem over which we are powerless. Of course, there are times in a person's life when he or she cannot or will not admit that. It is a breakthrough to admit that we cannot conquer a problem on our own.

AA then stresses that our Higher Power can set us free. The term "Higher Power" is used in order to reach people who may not belong to any religion or believe in God. For Christians, we realize that the Higher Power is God, and we reach out to one of the persons of the Trinity. And so, the 12-steps approach leads those affected by addiction to turn to God and to trust the power of God to free them from what has rendered them powerless.

AA is a group process, not a "me and God" approach. So there are regular group meetings, the commitment to honesty and confidentiality, and the need for a person in the recovery process to have a sponsor who is also in the recovery process. A person in the AA process is challenged to internally name the people they have hurt, to make amends and to tell the story (to confess) to another. People in the AA process are called to continue to deepen their relationship with God (or their Higher Power) and to do all they can to help others and to share the message of hope they have been experiencing.

Lives and families have been ruined by addictions; we are in the midst of what has been labeled the "opioid epidemic". Let us pray together with those who are grieving and those who are struggling and those who seem to be lost. With prayer, with God and with good people who acknowledge their brokenness, there is hope. Our prayers and support shine rays of hope. ♔

# CHAPTER 13

*Dark Night of the Soul:*

BULLETIN — December 13, 2020

This Monday we celebrate the feast day of St. John of the Cross, sixteenth century Spanish mystic who has given us the spiritual concept of the *Dark Night of the Soul*. The dark night of the soul frees many people from illusions, delusions and confusion. And yet the dark night is a time of mystery, obscurity and at times internal angst.

What we thought we knew is revealed as shallow. The way we have perceived God is revealed as not deep enough. The way we prayed is immature and futile. The way we understood our lives is revealed as too narrow. Our sense of inner peace and self-satisfaction are exploded.

The dark night is a kind of purgatory on earth, a purging of our illusions, delusions and confusions so that there can be a more clear and more true illumination of God, our lives, and our relationship with God and others.

Gerald May describes the dark night of the soul having two expressions. The dark night of the senses is a time of feeling disoriented, a time of focusing on unanswerable internal questions, guilt-inducing experiences, bad memories and personal inconsistency. But there is some sense of hope for a return to internal equilibrium. The dark night of the spirit engenders more a feeling of desolation, barrenness, emptiness, meaninglessness and abandonment. There is a basic feeling of shame, tiredness, dread, the inability to find words for the experience, and a sense of powerlessness. The dark night of the senses is like being lost in the woods at night; the dark night of the spirit is like being lost in a stark desert.

But prayer is still possible in every aspect of the dark night of the soul. We come to God the best way we can. We wait. We peel away some of the pretensions of righteousness and we come to God as vulnerable and human as we are. We show up...we wait...we pray for patience. We work at our prayer, we look for better ways to pray. We search the scriptures and the lives of the saints for models of those who have made this journey through darkness. But we often pray without words. We trust that God is with us whether the dark night brings misery, flatness, curiosity or hope.

Victor Parachin writes that our internal darkness leads us to yield control of our lives, heightens our sense of compassion for others, opens our eyes to God in new ways, leads us to deeper faith, and teaches us to value the light.

This Sunday is December 13. In other years on December 13, the church celebrates the feast of St. Lucy...the patroness of sight, the patroness whose very name means light. I believe it is a blessed coincidence that the feasts of Lucy and John of the Cross are on consecutive days.

The winter months are always the darkest times of the year. The additional factor of the pandemic makes it even darker. The feast of John of the Cross reminds us that God is still at work in these dark days of the pandemic; but we also need to do our work to keep ourselves and others safe and to hear and share God's words of hope. The darkness will not last forever; the light is coming; the one who is the LIGHT OF THE WORLD is coming. Lucy reminds us to trust the light, to be both patient and alert as we live and give hope. ♛

# CHAPTER 14

*Our Missionary Diocese:*

Many of you have asked about the Lexington Catholic bus which is parked outside of Church as the 11:15 a.m. Sunday Mass concludes. Lexington Catholic High School has generously made it available for a city-wide ministry to Congolese Catholics who have no other transportation to Mass. Their Catholic faith and attendance at Sunday Mass is very important to them. The eight parishes in Lexington have teamed up to financially sponsor the expenses related to this bus ministry. On Sunday the bus has three different pick-up areas, and three different destinations. A group is brought to Mary Queen of the Holy Rosary for their 8:15 a.m. Mass and other classes and socialization; our group is brought here for the 11:15 a.m. Mass (really at 10 a.m. for religious education, community building, etc.) and the third group is taken to U.K.'s Newman Center for the 5 p.m. Mass and socialization at the Spaghetti dinner after Mass. Plans are in the process for a monthly Congolese Mass on Sunday afternoons at St. Peter Claver. Many of the Congolese refugees have seen their families torn apart by violence and terrorism. Many have spent years in refugee camps. Their faith has sustained them during these times of chaos and fear. They have come to Lexington with a hope for a fresh start in life. We are called as a Church to do all we can to help the refugees from the Congo...and all other refugees to begin anew. One important aspect of this ministry is our bus ministry.

> *The mission of Lexington Catholic High School is to develop men and women whose lifestyles, decisions and spiritual depth will make a difference.*

As I reflect on Lexington Catholic, I realize that this is the beginning of the week of spring break for the students from Lexington Catholic in addition to the students from our school. It is always important to offer our appreciation to the faculty and staff of Lexington Catholic. But it is also important to express our encouragement to our parish's Lexington Catholic students who are working to develop their talents and preparing to live their faith in such a way that they can truly be leaders in our world. The mission of Lexington Catholic High School is to develop men and women whose lifestyles, decisions and spiritual depth will make a difference. We often see a high school publicized for sports, the fine arts, or other noteworthy accomplishments. But also Lexington Catholic students need to be commended for their dedication to community service, spiritual growth, and their commitment to live the Catholic way of life.

The parishes which have students at Lexington Catholic realize that their families are making sacrifices to send their sons and daughters there. We offer a tuition subsidy to every student's family which is active in our parish. This subsidy comes from our operating income, an income generated by our parishioners, young and old, whether you have, had or will have children at Lexington Catholic or not. Such is our belief in the value of the education and formation which Lexington Catholic High School provides. Lexington Catholic High school is part of the ministry of every Catholic parish in Lexington. ♛

This Sunday we celebrate Mother's Day. It is good for all of us to look back on our lives and to give thanks for the blessings our mothers have been to us. We pray in a special way for all those whose mothers have died over this past year. We also pray in a special way for all the women who have given birth over this past year, especially those who have had their first child.

Our mothers have often been key teachers and examples as we learn the teachings of the Church, the ways of compassion, and the importance of daily prayer. Our mothers very often console us with their gentleness but also guide us with their strength and determination.

This month as we focus on Mary the mother of Jesus, we trust in her guidance and example for all women, how she helps us to be faithful to and follow the way of Jesus, and the power of her prayers for us.

There are some situations where it is difficult to have a joyful memory of a mother. We pray for the healing that is necessary in these situations...and particularly for the wisdom to understand the reasons for whatever problems exist. We pray that those who feel resentment or wounded will be freed. Sometimes it helps to talk to a professional, to a minister, or to a trusted friend. Sometimes it helps to reach out to Mary, Our Blessed Mother.

I recall the Mexican families I knew when I ministered in Morehead. The mothers were very dedicated to their faith and dedicated to passing on their faith to their children. I saw the high level of family values in many Mexican families. And I shared their frustration as the women with very little facility in English tried to communicate their spiritual and religious concerns to me, who spoke no Spanish. Sometimes another older child, or another mother would have to be the spokesperson, but that was far from the best way. The situation was not solely the Mexican lady's problem...it was a problem we shared.

It is a good thing that the men preparing for the priesthood today are required to learn Spanish. (Father John has Mass in Spanish twice a month in Richmond.) Even this week, as the priests of our diocese will be away at our annual convocation, the focus of our seminars will be on ministry to immigrants and refugees. In our diocese the population of Latino Catholics is growing. Our suburban parish of Christ the King is not too often directly impacted...but we are called to be inclusive and welcoming, especially at the Diocesan events which are multi-cultural. I am very glad that our grade school and Lexington Catholic have strong Spanish departments.

> *With the strong devotion that so many Latino Catholics have to Mary, we are united and fortified as we walk together as members of the same Church...*

With the strong devotion that so many Latino Catholics have to Mary, we are united and fortified as we walk together as members of the same Church, moving towards the day when the rainbow of our various cultures will be even more beautiful.

This weekend I will be in Hershey, Pennsylvania, at St. Joan of Arc parish. I will be preaching at all six of their Masses this weekend and making an appeal for our missionary diocese of Lexington. Please keep me in your prayers. Priests, deacons and lay ministers from our diocese go around the country and make such appeals on an annual basis every summer. For instance, Deacon John Brannen has been to parishes in Rhode Island and St. Louis this summer. These mission appeals provide much-needed support for the missionary ministry of our diocese.

Earlier this summer, Christ the King hosted the director of the Maryknoll Lay Volunteers as he made a mission appeal here. Regardless of a parish's size, all parishes in the U.S.A. host a missionary appeal speaker on an annual basis. This helps all Catholics throughout the country to embrace the missionary aspect of our Church. It will be good to go to Hershey; it is part of the Diocese of Harrisburg, where Bishop Gainer is serving. His understanding of and dedication to our missionary ministry is one reason why his diocese has prioritized the inclusion of missionary appeals from the Lexington Diocese.

Whenever I make an appeal, I try to focus on Kentucky's Appalachia. Every city has an inner-city with its poverty and violence; every city has refugees and immigrants; Kentucky's Appalachia is unique. Eastern Kentucky is beautiful, and it is home to many beautiful and successful people. And yet the statistics do paint a challenging picture.

The territory of our diocese encompasses 50 counties, 40 of these are Appalachian counties. In many of these counties, the Catholic population is less than one percent. When I served in Morehead, part of my responsibility was Menifee County. There are less than a dozen Catholics in that county. In Appalachia, there are many Christians; but 60 percent report that they do not belong to any church. The Catholic Church is committed to have a parish or mission in every county in Appalachia. Yet many small congregations cannot provide the just financial support for a priest or lay minister. Our Mission Appeal provides financial assistance for those in Appalachian ministries.

The missionary work of the Church in Appalachia includes sharing the Good News of the Catholic Church and breaking down some of the prejudicial barriers and nurturing the faith of those who are members of the small congregations...But it also includes addressing the many socio-economic and health needs of the people of Appalachia.

The per capita income of the people of Eastern Kentucky is among the lowest in the nation. There is vast unemployment, there are not enough jobs, and many people are re-locating out of the area. The problems of drug, alcohol, pain-killers, obesity, and poor health habits are significantly above the national average. Education and the stability of marriages are also victims of the area's problems. The Church's missionary ministry includes charity, advocacy, and seeking to empower those who are enmeshed in the cycle of poverty.

Whenever I make a mission appeal for our diocese, I seek to tell the "Eastern Kentucky story" rather than sensationalize. I ask for a generous response to the collection, but I also encourage mission trips, adopting a parish or mission, and prayers...even as I offer the gratitude and prayers from the people of our missionary diocese. ♛

On behalf of our parish and the brothers and sisters who have been met, loved and helped by the A.B.L.E. volunteers who were in Eastern Kentucky last week, I offer our gratitude.

This weekend I will be away as I will be preaching at all the Masses at St. Catherine Church in Ithaca, New York. The focus of the preaching will be an appeal for support from the parishioners for the missionary ministry of our diocese. Two weeks from now, I will also be making a Mission Appeal at St. Paul's parish in Colorado Springs. Annually, many of the priests, deacons, religious, and lay ministers serving in our diocese make similar trips to generate support for our Mission Diocese.

The Church in the USA has a commitment that every parish, no matter what its size, receives a Mission Appeal every year. It is a reminder of the missionary context of our Church, an invitation to offer assistance, and an opportunity to broaden our vision of the Church's ministry. Our message is one that seeks financial support, but also seeks prayer, volunteers, connections, and offers a bit of education for those who live in different parts of our country.

Our diocese embraces Eastern Kentucky's Appalachia. Of the 60 parishes in our diocese, 40 of them rely on external funding to meet their expenses. Money generated by the appeals goes into the Diocesan Mission and Ministry Program, which offers over $1 million annually for parishes, schools and outreach ministries in the mountains.

Just about every diocese in our country has inner city poverty, unemployment, and challenges in offering ministry to migrants, immigrants and refugees. So also does the Lexington Diocese. But we have an additional challenging environment.

Catholics are three percent of the population in our diocese. Even in Lexington, we are a much smaller percentage of Catholicism than in many metropolitan cities. In many Appalachian counties, Catholics are less than one percent of the population. Additionally, in Eastern Kentucky, where most everyone identifies themselves as Christian, 60 percent of the people report that they do not belong to any church.

Eastern Kentucky has some of the poorest counties in our nation. Unemployment rates run to 25 percent or more. Minimum wage jobs are the norm. Poverty afflicts over 30 percent of the population. Educational attainment is low, with over 75 percent of people over the age of 20 lacking a high school diploma. Health issues are rampant, and access to health care professionals is well below the national average.

It is important not to stereotype, but the statistics do paint a troublesome picture. Appalachia is a land of beauty, of ruggedness, and of fascinating history but it is also a land where much of the natural beauty and proud spirit have been devastated. It is a beloved home for many people. The place of roots is very important to many people who have grown up in Appalachia. We desire to share the Good News of Jesus and the Good News of the Catholic Church. And so Appalachia is also our home, it is part of who we are as a Diocesan Church...and with all its majesty and all its challenges, with all its losses and all its grace, Appalachia is a blessing for us. ♙

# CHAPTER 15

## *It Is a Large World:*

BULLETIN — July 16, 2017

BULLETIN — July 21, 2019

BULLETIN — November 8, 2020

I am not aware of a recruitment poster for the priesthood which says, "Become a priest of the Diocese of Lexington, and see the world." If such a poster would be developed it would be true, even if it would apply to someone like me who has rarely traveled outside the USA. Ministry in the Lexington area has expanded to include ministry to Hispanic and Congolese Catholics, in addition to many other people born in other countries.

Sometimes, it feels like the world is coming to me. I realize that I have lived in the same rectory and worked with ten different men from other countries. I have either served with them as fellow priests on the same pastoral staff or else I mentored them as they were in a seminarian internship or an orientation program. In every case, I learned very much about our world and our World Church. The nations of origin for these men includes Vietnam, Nigeria, the Congo, Sri Lanka, Ireland, two priests from different parts of India, two priests from Mexico, and now Father Mark, from Kenya.

Each of these men has his own story; a story that often includes hardships, national chaos and terrorism. Very often, they have had to work to improve their English and to understand the U.S. approach to parish life. Sometimes they have needed to work their way through some stereotypes about the American way of life. They have made some adjustments to American food and also offered some new aromas and recipes to the rectory.

> *History speaks of missionaries who converted many people not just by their verbal communication but also by their good works and the power of their observable faith.*

I have traveled a few times to other countries. I can only speak the English language. I feel very vulnerable when on my own in another country. I admire these men who know several languages, who adapt quickly, and who have a joyful sense of adventure. Very often they speak of the large number of priests and seminarians in their home country. It is a reminder that the Church is growing in countries which we regard as still developing, even as there has been some downward trend for the Church in the Western World. Some of the men I have known come as missionaries to the United States, realizing the need we have for more priests, but also the need we have for evangelization that confronts the downside of our culture.

History speaks of missionaries who converted many people not just by their verbal communication but also by their good works and the power of their observable faith. I believe that this is the on-going blessing of our international priests...they will touch many lives by their humility, their transparent faith, and their generous kindness. In some ways, we are the hosts and offer hospitality and a welcome...but in many ways we are blessed by the gifts of their witness and faith, their kindness and compassion, and by the way they open for us windows into a larger world. ♛

The Book of Job describes the crisis of faith of a good man whose name was Job. Job was suffering mightily. He realized he did not deserve this suffering. It made no sense to him. He was angry at God for allowing so many bad things to take place. Job talked to God and honestly told God what he was feeling and asked God to explain why this was going on. God eventually responded and challenged Job to remember some of the fundamental mysteries of life...the paradoxes of where there is good and bad; where there is beauty and ugliness; where there is harmony and violence; where there is undeserved suffering and undeserved blessings.

It is all part of an awesome mystery...in chapters 38 and 39 God refers Job to the sun, the moon and the heavens and then God names some of the diversity of the animal kingdom...mountain goats, wild horses, oxen, cattle, ostriches, hawks, eagles, lions, crocodiles, ravens, hippopotamuses...and God asks Job if he can explain their differences, their personalities, or their very existence. Job is reduced to silence as he comprehends that he cannot explain the mysteries of life. Then he realizes that God is in control, God is good, and God will work out everything for the good. Job declares his faith and humbly opens himself to God's next mysterious step.

One aspect of Vacation Bible School is to nourish the seeds of faith in our children so that they can have the faith and patience of Job as they encounter life's difficult mysteries in the course of their lives. This week's Vacation Bible School will refer to many of the of the majestic, curious and powerful animals which are part of our world. We are reminded that life can feel like a zoo, a safari, a hunt, or being hunted, and we are reminded of the importance of freedom for all of God's creatures, so that we can live with our own blend of mild control and wild spontaneity.

When we visualize the animal kingdom's royalty, we often visualize Africa. Our parish has sponsored a mission in Ghana. We heard last weekend of Sister Pat's missionary ministry in Zimbabwe. We are served by Father Mark from Kenya and Father Damian from Nigeria. We are hosting an ESL class for Congolese refugees. Last Saturday I celebrated a wedding here at the cathedral for a Congolese couple; I can't really say that I danced, but I did draw from my somewhat dormant sense of rhythm with some swaying moves during some of the singing. I am grateful for that.

As our minds and hearts move to Africa, I suggest that we renew our understanding of African geography, that we review the sad history of slavery and colonialism, and that we do not forget the lack of food, clean water, and civil order within many of the countries of Africa. Also, we are called to gratitude for the fertile Catholic faith among many people in Africa. The volume of vocations in Africa to the priesthood and religious life is a blessing to our world.

I invite you to keep our children and their Bible School teachers and staff in your prayers this week. I invite you to find ways to encounter our brothers and sisters in the Lexington community who are natives of Africa. I invite you to our Bible School closing celebration on Friday evening and to our welcoming receptions for Father Damian next Sunday following our three morning Masses. ♛

This weekend the Church asks us to open our hearts to the needs of the Church in Africa in such a way that we offer support by our prayers and by our financial support through the second collection.

Christ the King volunteers have done much mission work of construction, faith sharing and encouragement in the community of Assassan, Ghana and the development of the ministry of our sister parish of Christ the King. And yet, over and over, our volunteers report that they believe that the spirit of joy and faith offered by Assassan's villagers has given them more than they could have imagined. .

A friend who is a religious sister in the Congregation of Divine Providence spent a summer a few years ago teaching English to sisters of her order who were members of the Madagascar Province. She was struck by the joy and deep faith of the sisters she met in Madagascar. The Sisters of Divine Providence are a group whose numbers are dwindling and who do not have many young sisters or women in formation in either the U.S. or in France, their country of origin. But the province of the sisters in Madagascar is robust and growing and has many younger women among the professed and in formation.

Father Mark, from Kenya, and Father Damian from Nigeria have touched many lives in their ministry here at Christ the King. Our local African refugees, comprised primarily of men, women and children from the Congo, have developed a strong community and have inspired many of us by their faith, their joy, their industriousness, and their choir. Many of them have seen terrible violence in their home communities and have lost loved ones to the terrorism which is part of everyday life, and many have spent prolonged periods in refugee camps.

Africa has been evangelized by Christians who came with the colonizers and profiteers from the Western World who came to take resources from the land and often took dignity and freedom from the people. The Catholic Church also brought missionaries who established schools, hospitals and social service agencies, in addition to parishes and outposts. Catholic colleges, seminaries and convents were established. More and more the bishops of African countries are natives. Seminaries and convents are full; Africans are now coming as missionaries to the Western World.

Africa is very important to the future of the Catholic Church. One prediction is that in our lifetimes, the number of Catholics in Sub-Sahara Africa will be 40 percent of Catholics in the world. It has been speculated that the number of Catholics in both Nigeria and the Congo will outnumber the number of Catholics in the U.S.A.

African countries still have their villages; but there also large metropolitan areas which rival the size, complexity and inner-city issues of any mega-city throughout the world. There remain many social needs; there is much migration; there is great poverty: many people suffer from food shortages, and illness, and many areas lack a strong medical system. The Church is there to offer ministry, service and justice. The Church is often a target for repression and violence in many African countries where greed, racial prejudice, tribal rivalries, and oppressive dictatorships plague the lives of good people.

Of course, we have our local needs. Today's collection is an opportunity to stand with the people of Africa and support pastoral projects which this continent so needs. Please be generous today. ♛

# CHAPTER 16

*Mary:*

BULLETIN — May 8, 2016

BULLETIN — March 21, 2021

I have been inspired by our recent celebrations of First Holy Communion to go back to the time when I was a little boy. I recollected how my brother and I would cut a side out of an oatmeal box, wrap the box in aluminum foil, and then place a statue of Mary inside. The shrine would then rest on top of a bookcase in our hallway leading from the kitchen to the living room. We would then place next to the shrine a vase or two of fresh roses from the garden in our side yard.

May is the month of the Blessed Virgin Mary. Many of us have a devotion to Mary. Scholars suggest that Mary conveys a more tender and feminine persona than any of the Three Persons of the Trinity. As the mother of Jesus and the Queen of Heaven and Earth, Mary has an exalted place in Christian spirituality and provides a gentle access into the Transcendent.

Mary is a model for us as a woman of faith, a woman who taught Jesus, and later learned from and followed Jesus. Mary ministered to the apostles and disciples of Jesus. She was a woman of courage and compassion. As the Pieta, she knows the anguish of grieving mothers and the mothers of prisoners; she knows the fear and uncertainty of unwed mothers; but she also knows the joy of mothers whose children are successful and women loved by their husbands. Mary exemplifies a spirit of inner peace as her son mysteriously developed.

*The Madonna of the Book by Sandro Botticelli*

Mary is not a mother who will manipulate Jesus to do our whims. We ask Mary to pray for us. She helps us to be honest and humble in our petitions to God, to persevere in our prayer, and to accept the will of God. Mary guides us to make good decisions, to see the needs of others, and to live as people of mercy.

Many people's lives have been changed by pilgrimages to the site of Marian apparitions. No woman has been the subject of more art than Mary. The Hail Mary mantra within the rosary connects us with Mary as we meditate on the mysteries of the life and ministry of Jesus and our own lives.

The crucifix above our altar portrays Jesus giving his beloved disciple and his mother to one another's care. This past Friday, Bishop John presided at our Marian coronation with our school children.

During May, it is good for us to reflect in a special way on the many dimensions of Mary and allow God's Spirit to develop our devotion. ♛

One of the Lenten devotions which so many of us find to be meaningful is the prayer revolving around the Stations of the Cross. The stations originated as stopping points in the streets of Jerusalem for pilgrims who had a desire to walk the path of Jesus and to pray with a vision of the various aspects of the ordeal that Jesus experienced. As time transpired and many people were willing but unable to make the journey to Jerusalem, stations of the cross were erected on the land of cathedrals and churches. Eventually, they were hung on the inside walls of churches and people could make their devotional walk from station to station.

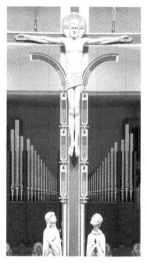

A frequent sung refrain with the stations is focused on the Blessed Mother..."At the cross her station keeping, stood the mournful mother weeping, close to Jesus to the last." There is a special anguish when any mother sees her son suffer and die unfairly; and yet Mary also stayed with Jesus and was faithful even as she was caught in the vortex of the mystery of God's Will for humanity's redemption.

Among the 14 stations is the fourth, where Jesus meets his mother. We can only imagine the pain she felt as she encountered her son who was moving forward with so much pain and resolve. We can only imagine all the thoughts and memories and prayers which went through her head and heart. We can only imagine her tears and her sense of helplessness. What did she say to Jesus...what could she say....

The 13th station depicts Jesus being taken down from the cross and placed in the arms of his mother. Those arms which once cradled the newborn babe in the

*Photo by Maureen Guarnieri-Yeager*

manger, those arms which hugged his day after day as a young boy, those arms which were wrapped around Joseph as they enjoyed their boy's special moments of achievement, those arms which had been raised countless times in prayer to the Holy Spirit, now they held the body of her son. Those hands which had cooked and baked and sewed and tousled her son's hair and pointed out first words to read and write and which had bandaged growing up hurts, those beautiful hands could do nothing now but hold and reverence the lifeless body of her son.

Above our altar is a crucifix which commands the attention of many people who come into the cathedral. It is Jesus on the cross...giving his mother and the disciple whom he loves into one another's care. Theologians suggest that the Beloved Disciple is kept anonymous for a good reason...the Beloved disciple represents you and me. We are beloved disciples...as disciples we are still learning how to be apostolic and yet we are cherished by God and we are called to care for Mary and for all who grieve and also to care for the Church of which she is the mother.

And as beloved disciples, we can trust that even more so, Mary will care for us...whatever brings us sorrow, Mary will understand and care for us with compassion....In effect, Mary is our mother and the words of Jesus from the cross clarify and intensify that relationship.

The question posed by the Good Friday hymn, "Were you there when they crucified my Lord?" receives its answer as we gaze at and ponder the message of the Crucifix above our altar. ■

# CHAPTER 17

*Mother's Day:*

BULLETIN — May 10, 2020

BULLETIN — May 9, 2021

I finally broke down and took a joy ride. Not an errand, not a ministerial call...just a ride through some of my favorite horse farm roads. I did not turn on the radio nor did I play music; it was just a time to get out on a beautiful spring day and to feel free. And, as seems to be happening more and more to so many of us, my thoughts and memories took me to places and people from the past.

I remembered the drives I used to take with my mom. "Mom, you want to go for a ride." She loved it. We would drive into the country, with no destination. I just did not want to come home on the same route we took on the way to the turn around place. Sometimes we had some good talks; but most of the time she fell asleep within 10 minutes.

Mom never drove. She once asked me to teach her how to drive...or maybe I talked her into it. I gave her one lesson. I am not sure whose emotions got riled the most. She did not wreck the car I had recently bought. Mom never drove.

I have one brother, John, who is a year older than me. When we were six and seven, our father suddenly died. Mom faced the crisis of raising her sons. She took care of us. Her aging mother was also living with us. Even though grandma contracted "hardening of the arteries", mom took care of her mother and grandma lived with us till her death.

*Photo by Maureen Guarnieri-Yeager*

Mom was determined to stay at home and guide her sons as we grew up. So she did not look for a job outside the home. She got a job as a typist and clerk for a large company in Cincinnati. Every Monday, a fellow worker or Aunt Edna, would drive mom to her company's office and she would deliver the past week's work and pick up the work for that week. Mom had an office in her bedroom. She typed and filed seven days a week and kept house and guided her two sons through grade school and high school. Her office overlooked the one-way street where we often played; in a corner of her bedroom was a stand and cage where the family canary would sing his sweet song.

When John and I were finishing high school, mom got a job as a secretary at Kenner Toy Company in Cincinnati. She rode the bus to work. It was fun to see her get out of the house and make new friends; we were proud of her.

One of her friends was an African-American lady. In the 1960s our

*(Continued on next page*

*(Continued from previous page)*

hometown was 100 percent white; in that volatile era of prejudice, there was fear of integration and riots. I was very proud of mom when she invited her friend to visit at our home.

We lived a block and half from our parish Church. We would often walk to Church together. Mom had a piano at home. She loved to play the piano and to sing. When she sang in Church she was really loud. As a typical teenaged boy, I was not always proud of her when she was singing so loudly in Church. Probably I have inherited a gene for loud singing in Church.

Church, faith and prayer was very important to her. I am sure that as she coped with her grief about her husband and her worries about her sons, her relationship with God and the Church were keys to her strength and good decisions. She regularly participated in our parish's annual women's retreat at Marydale.

In grade school and high school I would occasionally give hints that I felt a call to become a priest. (There were also some hints that I could become a person in need of a priest.) Throughout this discernment process my mother was encouraging, of course hopeful, but more than anything, she wanted her sons to be happy, to grow into good men. On mom's dresser in her bedroom she constantly burned a vigil light for her sons. It was electric; so it was lit 24/7. She just wanted us to follow God's will.

Following his time in the Air Force, my brother had an interesting career of work, entered the Sacrament of Marriage with his wife Ann, and had three children and now three grandchildren. I became the priest I am today as I am presently serving you.

Mom's remains rest in a cemetery in Northern Kentucky, next to her beloved husband's remains. Their gravesite is often a destination spot for John and me to pray. We trust that mom is still watching over us, still praying for us, still loving us. We are proud of and grateful for the work she has done as mother and friend and woman of faith. ♛

Today we celebrate Mother's Day. We give thanks for our mothers who have loved us and cared for us in wonderful ways. We give thanks for the many women we know who share life, love, wisdom and encouragement in ways that are motherly in an exemplary manner.

Let us hold in our hearts all mothers who have this year experienced the death of a child, no matter what the child's age. Their grief, especially with violent deaths and the ravages of the pandemic, needs to be respected.

Let us hold in our hearts those families where the mothering has been chaotic and not good. We never know what has contributed to the inner and interpersonal problems anyone has. Let us pray for understanding, for healing and safety for all involved.

Let us hold in our hearts those families where the mother has been affected by aging and illness and needs to be cared for in a way that calls for extra efforts from the adult children.

Let us hold in our hearts those mothers whose families have migrated from their home country because of injustice and violence and who are seeking a fresh start in a new country, but in so doing have become separated from one another. Let us pray for and work for reunions.

Let us hold in our hearts the mothers of criminals who have become incarcerated in our prisons. They know their sons and daughters are more than their worst crimes, they are confused about what went wrong, and they are afraid that their children have no future.

Let us hold in our hearts those mothers who are alienated from their children. We pray that the mothers never give up loving, even if it needs to be "tough love." We pray that they can find some common ground and some honest conversation that can bridge the gap.

Let us hold in our hearts those mothers whose hearts are broken because their children no longer practice their faith; may they trust that God's hand is still stirring.

Let us hold in our hearts mothers overwhelmed by the loss of a job, the pressures of child care, isolation, and the uncertainty of the future as they feel stuck in the cycle of poverty.

Let us hold in our hearts those women who yearn to be mothers, but for some reason have not been able to do so.

Let us hold in our hearts those mothers who are widows with small children. They miss the companionship, partnership and love of their husbands, they grieve and they simultaneously seek to care for their children who have their own grief.

Let us hold in our hearts all mothers who are widows as they miss the men whose life and love they have shared and who seek to find a clear and positive place within the lives of their adult children and their families.

Let us hold in our hearts those who are unwed mothers, those who have given birth when societal pressure suggests another "solution" to the unexpected pregnancy, and let us hold in our hearts those mothers who adopt and those who serve as foster parents.

Let us hold in our hearts those mothers who have chosen to abort and who now feel trapped in guilt and remorse; we pray that they can find the path to inner healing as they mourn and yet trust the power of Divine Mercy.

Let us hold in our hearts all mothers who are in a second marriage and therefore have two families and seek to have a place in each family and give love to her children and stepchildren.

Let us hold in our hearts all grandmothers who are raising grandchildren, often providing a home for their daughters. ♛

# CHAPTER 18

*Memorial Day:*

BULLETIN — May 28, 2017

BULLETIN — May 27, 2018

BULLETIN — May 30, 2021

This weekend we celebrate Memorial Day. It is a national holiday which was established during the Civil War to honor those soldiers who gave their lives in the midst of this struggle to define our nation. It is a day to solemnly reflect on the importance of military service.

Over the years I have been struck by the simple power of a prayer service at Camp Nelson and the other funerals where representatives of the military are present, when "Taps" is played, there is a 21-gun salute, and a flag of our country is presented to the veteran's family on behalf of our president and a grateful nation. Memorials to those killed in war have a special solemnity, as is evidenced by the Vietnam Wall in Washington, D.C. or the Vietnam Memorial in our own state capital.

We have family members and friends who truly came into their own during their time of military service. We also know people who have been scarred physically, emotionally and spiritually by the horrors they experienced in combat.

I am appreciative of the medical service provided by the V.A. Hospitals in town and all those who serve at both hospitals. I am appreciative of all those who reach out to veterans who are homeless. I am appreciative of the ministry of priests, rabbis and ministers who serve as chaplains with our military.

On this Memorial Day weekend, we pray for peace. Peace is more than the absence of war. Peace is justice, fairness, and a willingness to work internationally for the common good. We pray for those who work for justice and peace...for an end of war, an end of terrorism, for an end to the injustices which sow the seeds of war. We pray for military leaders who need to make life and death decisions. We pray for the safety of those who are non-combatants yet in the proximity of violent activities.

Those who serve in the armed forces have the charge to keep our world and our nation safe, just and peaceful. In our complicated world, this is a challenge. All who are in the armed forces need our prayers. ♛

Thank you to all who helped to organize and participated in the reception last Sunday for Father Mark and me in commemoration of our ordination anniversaries. It was a wonderful surprise. This anniversary has certainly offered the opportunity to give thanks for the blessings I have been part of in many people's lives over these 46 years. It has also provided the occasion to be thankful for Father Mark's ministry, as his ordination took place on May 20 of 2017. It is not always easy to adjust to all the challenges in the first year of priesthood, but he has responded with grace and generosity.

This Monday is another day of remembering. It is Memorial Day, a day when we particularly give thanks for those who have given their lives in order to preserve and nurture the best aspects of our national spirit and our freedom. Many will go to cemeteries as they visit the graves of loved ones. As I have presided at two burial services there in the course of five days, I am particularly cognizant this week of the subtle dignity of Camp Nelson Cemetery. I encourage you to simply take a drive out U.S. 27 and go through the cemetery, and/or to make a day trip to Camp Nelson Civil War Heritage Park as it reminds us of the training of African-American soldiers during the Civil War.

In my hometown of Bellevue, Ky., Memorial Day is always a day for a parade through the main streets of town. The parade includes veterans, city officials, local bands, Shriners in their funny little cars, little league ball teams, high school bands, scouts, churches, civic groups and just about anybody else who wants to be in it. Every year, citizens of Bellevue and people who grew up there line Fairfield Avenue (the "Avenue") to watch the parade and look for impromptu reunions.

When I served in Morehead, every Thursday morning before Memorial Day, Deacon Bill Grimes and I would go to the Owingsville City Park to bless the motorcycles of Vietnam Vets who had camped there overnight as they were travelling to the D.C. area on a memorial ride on behalf of prisoners of war and soldiers missing in action.

Throughout the country, Memorial Day is a reminder that summer is upon us...but even more so, it gives us the opportunity to give thanks for those who have given their lives for the values of our nation. As we live in delicate times, let us pray for peace in our world, peace in the hearts of those tempted to acts of terrorism, and peace in the dialogue of international leaders as they seek to cooperate in their efforts to keep our world safe.

One way to describe parish life at its best is the development of cherished memories. This Friday evening our parish pastoral council will gather here at Christ the King for an evening of prayer, reflection and planning for the upcoming year. But a big part of our meeting will be looking back on this past year, celebrating what we did well and building on what we have learned.

In the Church, our most Sacred Memorial is the Mass. We need more good men to serve as priests so that we and all our communities in our diocese will regularly have the blessing of Mass. This upcoming Saturday morning at 10:30 a.m. Bishop John will ordain to the diaconate three men who are on their way to the priesthood. I invite you to join us for this celebration as we give thanks for the call of God's Spirit and the generous response of these three men. ♛

Easter of 2020 was a day of dread and vague hope. No one could be in Church for Mass except the priest, lector, cantor, musician and the person who was running the live-stream. Even Father Ray could not come to Mass in church; he had a private Mass in the rectory on our dining room table. Everyone had a sense that we were living in a zone of danger. Family get togethers seemed to be out of the question. It was an isolated, lonely day. We had no idea what the duration would be, but we sensed that we were in for the long haul. We needed to watch the news; we needed to avoid the news.

On that Easter afternoon 14 months ago, I went to the Lexington Cemetery to be heartened by its beautiful spring flowers and foliage. It seemed like half of Lexington also had the same agenda. It was not a good idea to park and take a stroll. But the other side of the coin is that on that depressing Easter afternoon, the cemetery was seen not only as a place of beauty, but also a symbol of hope. The Good News of that first Easter morning took place in a cemetery!

This Monday is Memorial Day. It is a day when many people go to cemeteries and place flowers on the graves of their loved ones whose remains are in the cemetery. From a personal standpoint, I annually go to the cemetery in Northern Kentucky where my parents' remains rest beneath the earth and there is a sense that their spirits somehow feel my appreciation and prayers and that they in turn still have some parenting to give.

There is a special sacredness to every cemetery. Calvary, our Catholic cemetery, is less expansive than Lexington Cemetery, yet a walk through Calvary provides an historic overview of the life of the Church here in Lexington. Calvary is our cemetery; its beauty and maintenance are the result of the hard work of their staff and volunteers from our local parishes. I am always impressed by the professionalism and respect offered by the managers and field workers at the cemeteries. Theirs is a delicate and very important mission. The staffs of local cemeteries and funeral homes are very good; they are good to work with and they offer compassion and kindness to those who are grieving and often overwhelmed. We are grateful for their ministerial approaches to their work.

Memorial Day has a special context of remembering those who have given their lives in their service to our nation as members of the military. But we also give thanks in a special way for all those who have dedicated their lives to making our world more safe and just. And on this Memorial Day particularly, we remember those who have been victims of the pandemic and those medical professionals who have given their lives in the line of duty.

Memorial Day marks the beginning of summer. It is a day of picnics and family reunions. In my hometown, there is always a parade through the main streets of Dayton and Bellevue. This year, Memorial Day serves as one more benchmark that we are on our way through the pandemic.

The greatest memorial is our Eucharist. We remember that Jesus gave his life for us and shares his life at Mass. We have much to pray for this Memorial Day. I invite you to join Bishop John and us for our Memorial Day Mass on Monday at 10 a.m.! ♛

# CHAPTER 19

*Youthful Confirmations:*

BULLETIN — February 19, 2017

BULLETIN — February 16, 2020

This past Saturday at the 5 p.m. Mass 65 of our youth received the Sacrament of Confirmation. It was a glorious night for them as they culminated several months of preparation through study, prayer, service work and personal reflectiveness. Their parents were proud of them as they saw the readiness of their sons and daughters to continue growing in their faith. The mutual affection and respect of the youth and their sponsors was a source of inspiration for all at the Mass. All are appreciative of the dedication and the skill of their teachers, youth ministers and catechists. Our youth choir guided us in our sung prayer with a spirit that understood the blessing they were bringing and deepening. That evening we could sense the joy that Bishop John had in conveying this sacrament. Several people came to Mass last Saturday assuming it would be just like any other Saturday evening Mass. They were surprised, but were also caught up in the power of the Mass and the celebration of the sacrament.

The Sacrament of Confirmation is the third of the Church's Sacraments of Initiation. It is a conscious response to the Baptism which youth received at a much earlier age, generally as infants. Confirmation speaks of a person's readiness to live as a dedicated Christian, as a true disciple of Jesus. But also there is a change in the person which is more significant than his or her level of matured faith. With Confirmation, the Holy Spirit comes into a person's life and conveys a special gift, a gift articulated as the seven Gifts of the Holy Spirit. Confirmation is not just a rite of passage, but brings about a change. The Gifts of the Holy Spirit are bestowed and they can be drawn from or put into practice whenever a person needs them.

The Gifts of the Holy Spirit are wisdom, understanding, knowledge, prudence, courage, reverence and awe. The Holy Spirit inspires us to foster and employ these gifts; Confirmation acknowledges our desire and readiness to trust the power of the Holy Spirit's gifts. Confirmation is not the end of religious formation...in many ways it is a new beginning. No matter how long ago we were confirmed, it is good to review its meaning.

Today's Gospel passage closes with the injunction of Jesus to be perfect as the Heavenly Father is perfect. This injunction to be perfect has plagued many people who are a bit stuck in perfectionism. Over the years, word studies have suggested that Jesus meant "be made perfect...let your life be transformed by the hands of God"..."be complete"... "be committed to excellence"..."be a mirror of God's perfection"..."be perfectly present to God's Word"..."be compassionate".

Confirmation does not invite perfectionism, but does invite and EMPOWER everyone who has been confirmed to trust God's transformative power...to be the complete, whole and holy best version of our self...to be committed to excellence...to trust God's Light...to have a basic dedication to God's Word...and to live with consistent and dynamic compassion. ♛

Next Saturday at the 5 p.m. Mass, Bishop John will celebrate the Sacrament of Confirmation with the youth of our parish. The group is comprised primarily of eighth grade students from our school and our CCD/Youth Group program. It will be a special night for them. Their families are proud of them. Their parents see how their boys and girls are developing and traveling the delicate road to adulthood and making the transition from childish faith to faith that understands and integrates the meaning of discipleship.

It is also a special night for their catechists who have been teaching and guiding them this year and in the previous years to help them to arrive at this time in their lives when they are ready to receive and draw from the gifts of the Holy Spirit. Whether they are part of our school staff or parish staff, or volunteers, the members of our catechetical team are outstanding and they teach by word and by example.

It is a special night for the sponsors whom the youth have chosen. The sponsors are men and women that the youth look up to. They are people who live their faith in an exemplary manner. Our youth have chosen them because they know they can count on their prayers, supporting and mentoring.

As the teens have been learning and growing and seeking to pray better and to put their faith into action, their parents have been supportive, but in many cases, very involved, and they have experienced a renewal of their own faith. I offer a special note of gratitude to those parents who are not Catholic, but have been supportive of and encouraging the Catholic faith journeys of your children.

Throughout the years, there have been several different understandings of Confirmation.

First and foremost, Confirmation is a beginning more so than an ending. It is not the end of religious education and formation, but the beginning of living life in a way responsive to the Gifts of the Holy Spirit. As we experience Confirmation, it is the third step in the process of being initiated into the life of a follower of Jesus in the Catholic faith. At Confirmation, our youth are saying "yes" to their Baptisms — when they became members of the family and followers of Jesus. And they are saying "yes" to the Eucharist (and to Sunday Mass) as the Source and the Summit of their Christian lives.

Not too many years ago, Confirmation was referred to as making youth "soldiers for Christ". We seldom use that term any more, but Confirmation does remind youth of the importance of listening to God's call for them to have a mission in life.

The seven gifts of the Holy Spirit are wisdom, understanding, knowledge, courage, right judgement, prayerfulness, and reverential wonder. The Gifts are planted at Confirmation; the appreciation of the need for the gifts is planted; and the realization of God's desire to convey these gifts is highlighted at Confirmation. The belief in the power of the Holy Spirit to touch our lives and empower us to transcend our limitations is at the heart of Confirmation. We believe that the Gifts of the Holy Spirit will be the keys to our youth living with joy and making a difference in our world. ♛

# CHAPTER 20

*Priesthood:*

BULLETIN — October 23, 2016

BULLETIN — November 13, 2016

BULLETIN — October 18, 2020

Many of us know from our personal experience the value of a spiritual retreat. Priests, deacons, religious men and women have an annual retreat as part of our spiritual pilgrimages. All four of us priests who live in the rectory will be on retreat this week. Frs. Arock, Ray, John and myself will be at Saint Meinrad Archabbey from Monday till Friday along with Bishop John and most of the priests serving in our diocese. The Jesuit Order has its own system of annual retreats, so Fr. Gino will be staying at home and making his retreat at another time.

Priests usually go on retreat in one of three ways: 1) a directed retreat, meeting daily with a trained spiritual guide who suggests meditation topics; 2) a Spirit-led retreat with an emphasis on silence, solitude and trusting God's Spirit to provide direction; 3) a preached retreat, where a group pray and reflect in response to talks given 2-3 times daily by a retreat director (similar to a parish mission).

In our diocese, in odd years, priests individually choose the time, place and style of our retreat. In even years, like this year, our priests participate in a preached retreat with a large group of fellow priests from throughout the diocese. We count on parish life to continue for a week without our presence.

Most of us priests look forward to our annual retreat. It is a special time to be with Our Lord and a concentrated time to listen for the words that Jesus has for us at this season in our lives. It is also a time of prayerful camaraderie with our Bishop and fellow priests who share our commitment to and love for Jesus, who share our dedication to and history with the Church of Eastern and Central Kentucky, and who understand and appreciate our questions, doubts, and frustrations as well as support our joys, hopes, ideals, and faith. Retreat almost always has a strong element of rest, but occasionally evolves into a time of wrestling with the Lord and our personal and

> *Very often on a retreat, a priest evaluates his daily and weekly schedule, his relationships with friends, family and parishioners, and evaluates his vision, illusions, and sense of mission.*

societal demons. Very often on a retreat, a priest evaluates his daily and weekly schedule, his relationships with friends, family and parishioners, and evaluates his vision, illusions, and sense of mission. Strikingly, our retired priests place a high value on the retreat; it is a time when priests who are uncluttered with a job description can simply go deeper in their dedication to prayer, friendship with Jesus and care for the community of priests and the people we serve.

And so, as Frs. Arock, Ray, John and I will be on retreat, keep us in your prayers. You will be in our prayers.

One of the ministries within our parish's Spiritual Life Ministry is entitled *The Hands of Mary*. This group of parishioners is dedicated to praying for vocations to the religious life and priesthood. They offer support to those of us who are already clergy and religious, but also encourages men and women to consider living their lives as priests or religious. Last weekend we particularly focused on religious women and this weekend we focus on the priesthood.

This column today will offer a few reflections on the priesthood. As a Cathedral, we are the host for the ordination of men to the priesthood. We are very often a summer training ground for men who are in the seminary and on their way to priesthood. We are a large parish...always in a large parish here are some men who not only have "the right stuff" to be a good priest, but also are stirring internally with a discernment process. In a parish of our size, there are always a few men of a variety of ages who are wondering if God is calling them to be a priest...and also wondering if they can live this life in a good way. If you as a reader are considering the priesthood, please look up Father Gino, Father John, Father Ray or myself. Father Gino brings the perspective of a priest in religious life, Father John entered the seminary in his 40's, Father Ray once served as a vocation director and as a retired priest can draw from over 50 years' experience, and I have the perspective of over 40 years of ministry and the memory of deciding that God wanted me to be a priest when I was in early grade school.

> 66
>
> *A priest brings Christ into people's lives through the Sacraments, but also leads them to Christ by his demeanor and example of compassion. Priests lead by teaching, preaching and listening.*
>
> 99

A priest is a servant-leader. A priest is dedicated to prayer and yet always knows he is being called to another level of friendship with God. A priest brings Christ into people's lives through the Sacraments, but also leads them to Christ by his demeanor and example of compassion. Priests lead by teaching, preaching and listening. Some priests are extroverts; some are introverts. A priest loves people and yet challenges people to be faithful to the teachings of the Church. A priest helps people know what is most important. A priest is socially involved, but at peace with the solitude of his life. A priest, by choosing celibacy, gives testimony that a relationship with Christ is the most important relationship in life and that its joys will be sufficient. A priest is a minister of spiritual healing, but also a minister of healing and reconciliation in many other ways. A priest unifies the people he is serving and leading.

On this weekend dedicated to the priesthood, I ask your prayers for those of us who serve as priests and for all who are thinking and praying about a call to the priesthood. ♛

Every priest serving in our diocese is expected to make a retreat on an annual basis. It is usually from Monday through Friday. A retreat is designed to be a time of renewal, refreshment, and prayer. Most retreats are times of peace, but sometimes there needs to be some inner turmoil in addressing critical issues. This year our annual priests' retreat has been scheduled to take place this week at Saint Meinrad Archabbey in Southern Indiana. Because of pandemic restrictions, Saint Meinrad is closed to people who are not part of their day by day community. Some of our priests will still go on retreat this week as presentations will be offered through Zoom. Others of us will make our retreat at another time this year.

Retreats are valuable for anyone seeking to live a life of faith. Retreats have different themes and different topics for presentations. Two essentials of retreats are rest and silence; rest, so that the retreatant can have the energy to be open to the movements of God's Spirit (the Ultimate Retreat Director!) and silence, so that the retreatant can hear the unexpected Word of God. Most retreats take place in a beautiful natural setting so that the retreatant can appreciate God's handiwork.

For a priest, there are several topics which are always profitable to reflect on, to discuss with a retreat director, and about which to pray. I offer a short list of some of these themes.

1. The call and the second call...The mystery and the blessing of the call to the priesthood and how that call has been re-defined, refined and responded to over the years
2. Prayer and fidelity to prayer, and the need to make prayer a priority and the ways prayer habits develop. A priest on retreat often reaffirms the importance praying the breviary and other aspects of daily prayer. Retreat is often a time of dealing with difficulties in prayer; very often a priest on retreat prays very intensely.
3. A priest on retreat reviews his life as he seeks to live with faith, hope and charity. There is sometimes a need to work on some areas of doubt or struggles to believe; to grow as a person of hope who engenders hope in other people; and to review one's consistency in living as a person of compassionate service.
4. A priest is a man of relationships; with family members, friends, parishioners, fellow priests and special friends. Wherever there are relationships, there are times when problems have developed which need to be resolved in a way that is best for everyone involved.
5. A priest on retreat often prays about and considers some of the most important issues in the parish or other assignment where he is serving. Retreat is not a time for business, but often the critical issues of a parish are based on spiritual issues.
6. A priest on retreat also reflects on the Church, and all its greatness and all its flaws and how he fits within the structure of the very human, but very apostolic Church.
7. A priest on retreat often reviews the beauty and the power of the Eucharist and reflects on how best to lead the congregation in prayer at the Mass.
8. A priest on retreat often goes to confession and seeks spiritual direction, as he recognizes the healing and strengthening which this great sacrament offers.
9. A priest on retreat often reviews his role in the brotherhood of priests and the blessings he has received from other priests' friendship, encouragement and good example.
10. A priest on retreat often prays with particular passages of the Bible which present Jesus to him as he gives thanks for the love and leadership of Jesus and seeks to go deeper.

There are many more possible themes of a retreat, and many themes open to a myriad of important sub-themes...but this list offers to you a view of the importance of an annual retreat for a priest. Please pray this week for the priests who are on retreat. ♛

# CHAPTER 21

*Care of the Sick:*

BULLETIN — October 16, 2016

BULLETIN — December 2, 2018

Last weekend's celebration of the *Sacrament of the Anointing of the Sick* at the Sunday Masses touched many hearts, reminded us of the variety of ailments which, although not always obvious, are causes for serious concern, apprehensiveness, and suffering. It was encouraging to witness the reverence and the compassionate spirit as our congregations prayed with those who came forth for the anointing.

One of the most important ministries of any parish is the ministry of care for the sick. Our parish has a team of parishioners who regularly visit fellow parishioners who by illness are confined to their homes and who are residents at nursing home or rehab facilities. Our visitors bring kindness and friendship and they bring Christ present in Holy Communion. They provide a connection with the parish and with the Body of Christ.

> 66
>
> *In the bulletin is an emergency phone number for critical situations that call for as immediate a response as possible. We priests take "monthly shifts" carrying the emergency phone.*
>
> 99

Each of Lexington's eight parishes has a specific responsibility to provide pastoral care for specific hospitals plus specific nursing homes and residential care facilities. And so the clergy and lay volunteers from various parishes will visit our parishioners in specific institutions all around town. However, we clergy also are ready to visit our parishioners in whatever hospital or facility they are in. And we are also dedicated to making home visits. Sometimes we are not aware of a parishioner who needs a visit. Please let us know.

I am also aware that sometimes a person is not an active member of our parish or any other parish, but would like to see a priest. We priests are always ready to make this kind of visit also...never to force, but to be available for someone at an important time in their life and the their journey of faith. Please let us know.

In the bulletin is an emergency phone number for critical situations that call for as immediate a response as possible. We priests take "monthly shifts" carrying the emergency phone.

Both clergy and lay volunteers constantly report that ministry to those who are sick is an important way to give, but also this ministry has many unexpected blessings, as we meet people with great faith, courage and patience, as we are inspired by the fidelity of family members, and as we see health care professionals on many different skill levels who approach their work as ministry.

I offer my thanks to all who give of yourselves in caring for those who are aging, suffering or vulnerable. The prayers we share, the hope we share, the love we share brings us closer to Christ and the joy, strength and peace which the Lord's Providence offer us. ♛

This weekend we will be offering the Sacrament of the Anointing of the Sick at all our Masses. Fathers Mark, Kiran and I will be at all the Masses and we will be joined by several other priests who will be helping with the administration of the Sacrament. It is a wonderful experience for the Sunday Mass assembly to witness and pray with and for brothers and sisters who are receiving this great sacrament. Those who wish to be anointed will be invited to the Communion railing and one of us priests will lay our hands on their foreheads and then anoint their foreheads and the palms of their hands. (If you or a loved one is unable to come forward, one of us priests will come to you.) The Sacrament of the Anointing of the Sick conveys the healing power of Jesus and the Church for those who are afflicted with a serious health condition. It is not just for people who are in danger of death. If a person has been previously anointed and the illness or treatment is in "another chapter", it is appropriate to receive the Sacrament of the Sick again.

The Sacrament of the Anointing of the Sick is for baptized members of the Church who have reached the age of reason. Spiritually, it fits within the context of receiving the Sacrament of Reconciliation and then receiving Holy Communion. In many cases, it deepens the healing process related to intercessory prayer for healing.

The Catechism of the Catholic Church names four effects of the celebration of this Sacrament.

It is a particular gift of the Holy Spirit and so conveys the grace of strength, peace and courage to overcome the difficulties which accompany serious illness or the frailty of old age. This gift of the Holy Spirit renews trust and faith in God and strengthens against the temptations to discouragement or anguish. This assistance from God's Holy Spirit can also lead to a healing of the soul.

The Sacrament's grace leads a suffering person to be more closely united to the Passion of Jesus, in a way, to participate with the redemptive suffering of Jesus.

The person receiving this Sacrament, and thereby united with the Passion of Jesus, is able to make a difference for other people and for the Church. The Anointing not only forges a deeper union with Jesus, but facilitates a share in the sanctifying work of Jesus. As we offer up our sufferings, and as we live in a Christ-like manner even while suffering and facing fear and our limitations, we can make a difference in the lives of many people.

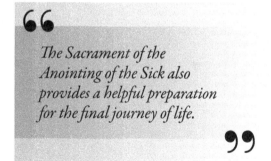

> *The Sacrament of the Anointing of the Sick also provides a helpful preparation for the final journey of life.*

The Sacrament of the Anointing of the Sick also provides a helpful preparation for the final journey of life. When anointed, we put our lives, our hearts and our souls in the hands of Our Lord, and we express our trust that God's grace will be enough for us while living on earth, while living in eternity, and in all the aspects of the time of transition from earth to eternity. ⚜

# CHAPTER 22

## *Father's Day:*

BULLETIN — June 16, 2019

BULLETIN — June 21, 2020

It is providential that we celebrate Father's Day on the Sunday which is the feast of the Holy Trinity. The relationship of God the Father with God the Son offers some ideals for fathering and leads us to specify some of the aspects of our own experiences of fathering for which we are grateful.

We define our mysterious God as Love; God is described by love. Theologians speak of the love that each person of the Trinity has for one another as the heart of the triune relationship. The Gospels record at the time of Jesus' baptism that God the Father declared his love for Jesus, "This is my Beloved Son in whom I am well-pleased." A good man who is a good father loves his children. It is parallel to the marital covenant...for better — for worse, in sickness and in health, in good times and in bad, for richer or for

*Holy Family by Francois de Poilly*

or poorer...all the days of our lives. Of course, love can be expressed in many ways...but the bottom line is love.

God the Father sent Jesus into the world to redeem us. A good father helps his children to grow into people who have a sense of mission in life. A good father also teaches his children to be resilient. In many cultures, a good father trusts the power of unpleasant rituals of passage which usher in adulthood. God the Father called for Jesus to give his life on the cross. God the Father, in raising Jesus from the dead, brought about the greatest act of resilience in the history of the world.

A good father has empathy. In the mystery of the Trinity, we can trust that God the Father felt with Jesus in his times of rejection, suffering, hope and joy. Jesus taught that he and his Father are one. In family life, the ideal is unity, a sense of oneness, a connection which is unbreakable. And yet, just as with the Trinity there are different roles, each person within a family needs the freedom to develop their own role in life.

God the Father loved the mother of Jesus. In fact, for Jewish people of faith like Mary, God the Father was the Person of the Trinity most known and prayed to. A good father loves his wife and does so following the example of God's love for Mary, God's choice of Mary, God's fidelity to Mary, and God's protection of Mary.

Jesus prayed to his Father and sought to know and do the will of God; and he did so because the Heavenly Father radiated goodness and wisdom. A good father on this earth radiates goodness and wisdom which children of all ages seek to draw from. The Father answered the prayers of Jesus with words of encouragement; so too, a good father on this earth offers encouragement and confidence that his children can navigate the challenges of life.

We wish all a beautiful day today. Even those men who are not biological fathers can generate life by the encouraging and life-enhancing spirits in which we live. May our prayers be punctuated by gratitude for the men who have believed in us, helped us to develop, and who give us life in many ways. ♛

This Sunday we celebrate Father's Day. Over the years, I have grown more and more comfortable being called "Father", even by men and women who are my age or older. This Father's Day, I'd like to share a few thoughts on some of the best qualities of a father.

A good father generates life. Of course, that is what makes a biological father. And yet there is more to generating life than being a partner in procreation. A good father, and a fatherly man, helps others to live well. This generally applies to his influence on people of the next generation...and most of the time especially to his children. A good father helps a person to really be alive, to live with joy and with happiness.

A good father offers encouragement. Advice and challenge and honest talking have their place, but encouragement and affirmation are so important for the development of children and those for whom a man has responsibility. In order to encourage, a man needs to observe and listen to the evolving stories of each person in the family.

A good father is faithful to his family. He is present and available, he makes his wife and his family his top priority, he makes the choice to be with them, he does all he can to express and share his love.

A god father realizes he has power. He does not need to be rich or physically strong, but he has power and honors that power and uses the power for good, and does not focus on his power. The power is one aspect of who he is, and particularly with his wife he shares that power. As the children grow into adulthood, a good father honors and respects the power that his children have.

A good father lives a principled life. He knows what is right and what is wrong, but he also realizes the individuality of his children and that they might have different tastes, opinions and priorities than his. Discussions and even debate help everyone to be more understanding of themselves and one another. A good father stays true to his principles, but also has a certain level of openness to diversity within the family...and he fosters that balance of principles and openness so that the rest of the family will relate to one another with respect.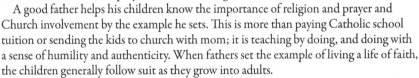

A good father knows himself and trusts the promptings of the Holy Spirit. He is a leader, but also a servant. He sets a good example by living his life with integrity, respect for others, and the courage to stand up for what is right. He is a man of faith, who knows the need for prayer and the Divine guidance which God can offer.

A good father helps his children know the importance of religion and prayer and Church involvement by the example he sets. This is more than paying Catholic school tuition or sending the kids to church with mom; it is teaching by doing, and doing with a sense of humility and authenticity. When fathers set the example of living a life of faith, the children generally follow suit as they grow into adults.

Catholic theology regards parenthood as evangelization, a prime way to pass on the faith, to form the children into disciples who will make the world a better place. The Rite of Children's Baptism has a blessing for both the mother and father. The text of the blessing for a father is, "God is the giver of all life, human and divine. May he bless you, the father of this child. You and your wife will be the first teachers of your child in the ways of faith. May you also be the best of teachers, bearing witness to the faith by what you say and do in Christ Jesus our Lord." ♛

# CHAPTER 23

## *Our Beautiful World/Laudato Si:*

BULLETIN — April 15, 2018

BULLETIN — September 1, 2019

BULLETIN — July 5, 2020

Only God knows what the weather will be like on the day you read this. Hopefully, spring will have finally spring. I am writing on the Monday morning after spring break. It is a morning so dark and cold that I passed on going out for a morning workout and instead decided to straighten up the office I have in the rectory. Basically that means organizing a stack of books between two bookends and putting magazines which I have finished reading into the recycle can. It is a step beyond re-arranging the deck chairs on the Titanic. Still, that is not a bad way to begin the day: to make a step into the zone of spring cleaning.

Spring offers a spirit of hope and new life; in many sports, spring is the season of preparing for the next season; spring is the season of planting and nurturing the seeds that will hopefully grow into beautiful and healthy flowers and plants.

In our parish's life, spring has much of that same character. It is a time of hope, a time of preparation, and a time of refreshment as we savor the results of what we have been doing through the year.

> **"** *We have much to celebrate, there are many challenges ahead of us, but my predominant feeling is one of gratitude for your generosity, your spirit and your love for our parish.* **"**

As we move towards May, we will be having elections for some new members of our parish's pastoral council and our parish's school council. Please keep in your prayers those who are coming forth as candidates and consider encouraging fellow parishioners to serve in these positions. Our councils provide a great service to our parish by their ministry, wisdom and love for our parish.

We are in the interview process with candidates for our parish organist/assistant music director and have postings for our business manager position and another member of our maintenance crew. Please keep us and all involved in your prayers so that this all goes smoothly.

We continue with our capital campaign and the need for more to step forth with donations and pledges. There are a variety of projects which are in various stages of their work and contract negotiations to prepare us for a summer of activity on our major projects of repair and renewal. We continue also to make progress in our weekly offertory collections, but have not reached our goal of every parishioner household giving an extra $10 per week. We have much to celebrate, there are many challenges ahead of us, but my predominant feeling is one of gratitude for your generosity, your spirit and your love for our parish.

Spring is horse racing season; many of us will enjoy the beauty and the drama at Keeneland. As the horses are running there is always a critical time towards the end of the race. It is time for a "kick", for the equine and human athletes to kick into the next gear and give their all. As we make our run through spring, the finish line of our Church year and fiscal year is June 30. Let's together do all we can to kick into the highest gear with our stewardship, our sense of evangelization, and our spiritual growth in the light of our encounter with the Risen Jesus. ♔

We live in a beautiful world. Recently I introduced the Arboretum to a friend who has lived in Lexington for some time, but had never been there. He loved the simple beauty and variety of plants, trees and flowers, and the sense of care that the Arboretum evokes and from which it benefits. During my vacation I took a contemplative stroll through Newport's Aquarium and was awed by the beauty of so many fish whom I had never heard of, fish who lived in waters in the vicinity of far-off countries. This summer, as we commemorated the 50th anniversary of the lunar landing, we were reminded of the mysterious extensiveness of our mysterious universe. Last weekend, as I preached at St. Michael's parish in Indianapolis, I spoke of the beauty of the mountains of Eastern Kentucky. Very often on my early morning walks and other exercise forays, I am touched by the beauty of the chirping birds, the majestic trees, and the opening sky.

And yet, we do not always care for and seek to protect God's creation. We often use our resources in a wasteful manner. Species of animals and plants are becoming extinct. The volume of uncared for and abused pets is scandalous. We live in a culture that fails to reduce the amount of waste which we generate. Our culture is reluctant to recycle. Climate change, with all its attendant natural catastrophes, is a reality which to a great extent is due to humanity's destruction of ecosystems. Our consumer culture places more value on the use of the earth rather than friendship with the earth.

From September 1 until October 4, (the feast of St. Francis) the Church is observing a season of creation. In 2015, Pope Francis wrote the challenging encyclical *Laudato Si* as a call to action and as an invitation to dialogue about the life-style changes we need to make.

In paragraph 2 of *Laudato Si*, Pope Francis writes "Our sister earth now cries out to us because of the harm we have inflicted on her by our irresponsible use and abuse of the goods with which God has endowed her. We have come to see ourselves as her lords and masters, entitled to plunder her at will. The violence present in our hearts, wounded by sin, is also reflected in the symptoms of sickness evident in the soil, in the water, in the air and in all forms of life. That is why the earth, burdened and laid waste, is among the most abandoned and maltreated of our poor."

The encyclical's final words are words of prayer from Pope Francis, "God of love, show us our place in the world as channels of your love for the creatures of this earth, for not one of them is forgotten in your sight. Enlighten those who possess power and money that they may avoid the sin of indifference, that they may love the common good, advance the weak, and care for this world in which we live. The poor and the earth are crying out. O Lord, seize us with your power and light, help us to protect all life, to prepare for a better future, for the coming of your Kingdom of justice, peace, love and beauty. Praise be to you! Amen" ♕

This weekend, a holiday weekend, offers a special time to celebrate our nation, our independence from any foreign country and the ideals that have defined our national character. We realize that we are not free from the threat of the coronavirus, we are not yet free from our nation's" original sin" of racism, nor are we free from the vituperative polarization that saps our spirit of unity. We need to be vigilant and dedicated to the protocols which keep others and ourselves safe; we need to listen to the stories of those victimized by racial prejudice as we work for justice and equity; we need to explore the grounds which have led so many people to extreme positions and we need to find common ground so that we can dialogue.

But this is a holiday weekend. It will be good to take a break...a safe break, a break with the right kind of social distancing, protection of self and others, wearing masks and sanitizing. The virus is still out there.

A drive through horse farm country, a small cookout with appropriate distancing, a hike in the Red River Gorge region might be the best way to celebrate our independence in this stage of our post-lockdown re-opening.

About 10 days ago, I went to Natural Bridge State Park for an evening hike, a night's rest in the lodge, and a hike in the morning. I took the long way home, traveling through the Nada Tunnel on Highway 77, following the meandering of the Red river into Menifee County and its county seat of Frenchburg.

We do live in a beautiful state. At Natural Bridge, the trees, the wildflowers, the chirping birds, the rock formations, the gentle morning sun, the mild temperature, the few billowing clouds reminded me how lovely our world and our state are. It was enjoyable to see a few other early morning hikers, ready to celebrate just being out in the fresh air...families and young friends, all of us bubbling with joy as we enjoyed being in the midst of God's marvelous creation. The staff at the lodge were all masked hombres, doing everything right to keep themselves and all of us safe. As careful as we need to be, such a short trip reminded me of the sacredness of life.

My mind tried to visualize the extensive logging work in the gorge area, the development of railroads for transporting the logs, the railroad company building the first lodge, and the work of the Civilian Conservation Corps to actually construct the park. I tried to visualize the many different species of animals who have their homes in the hills. And I imagined in awe on the centuries of Red River water cutting through the limestone hills and forming the gorge and the bridge.

It is always good to hike up to the bridge, to make it one more time through "Fat Man's Misery", and to take a few pictures from below and on top of the bridge. It is even more interesting to drive through the Nada Tunnel — going through I ask dramatically, "Why am I doing this?" and when through it, feeling very young, but also very relieved, and looking forward to a beautiful drive.

I refer you to the psalms, particularly, Psalm 104, as we all give thanks to God for creating such a wonderful world. Our world's survival depends on our stewardship of the world...our survival depends on what the world gives us. We and the world are interdependent rather than dependent or independent...so too, we and the people of our world are interdependent! ⚒

# CHAPTER 24

*Jesuits:*

BULLETIN — November 19, 2017

BULLETIN — July 28, 2019

This weekend we celebrate Father Gino in a special way and we give thanks for his many years of ministry here at Christ the King. Father Gino will celebrate our Sunday evening 5 p.m. Mass and we will have an Appreciation Reception in Hehman Hall following the Mass. Thanks to all who have helped to organize this event and provide our refreshments. The Parish Life Committee and their team of volunteers have been called upon more often than usual this fall, and they have always responded with skill and generosity. Thank you to all involved in the set-ups and working behind the scenes.

As we celebrate Fr. Gino we also recall the members of the Jesuit Order presently serving in Lexington...Frs. Bado, Bueter, and Von Kaenel, plus those deceased Jesuits whom we hold dear — Frs. Hank Kenny, Lou Lipps, and Bob Murphy.

For many years I was nourished by the spiritual direction offered by Fr. Lipps. I have often made my annual retreat at a center directed by Jesuits; in 1984 I made a 30 day retreat, guided by a Jesuit priest, and it was a very important step in my spiritual growth. With that limited background, I would like to offer some perceptions "from the outside" on the blessing that Jesuit priests offer to our Church and the people we serve.

In the aftermath of the Reformation, the Jesuit Order began. Their founder was St. Ignatius Loyola. He offered their services to the pope, to serve the Church in whatever way was needed in the post-Reformation period of re-building. At the time, the Church was sorely in need of solid scholarship and teaching, orthodox formation of those preparing to serve as priests, and a deepening of spirituality and prayer. The Society of Jesus, the Jesuits (S.J.) rose to the occasion and more...providing this kind of ministry in addition to a strong commitment to missionary ministry, caring for the poor and the sick, and generously responding to any need within the communities served by the Church.

When many people think of Jesuits, we rightly think of strong education...universities and high schools that have the Jesuit character. But also the spirituality of St. Ignatius is an even deeper foundation for every aspect of a Jesuit's ministry. Three aspects of Jesuit ministry stand out...

- A focus on knowing, encountering and following Jesus

- A trust that there is a path (spiritual exercises) to pray better and to discern the will of God

- A foundational belief that God can be found in all experiences, in all things, in all people

St. Ignatius had a beautiful prayer, "Take Lord, receive all my liberty, my memory, my understanding, my entire will, all I have and call my own. Whatever I have or hold, you have given me. I restore it all to you, and surrender it wholly to be governed by your will. Give me only your love and your grace and I am rich enough and ask for nothing more."

On behalf of all of us I express our appreciation for the unique and wonderful ways Father Gino has been sharing himself, Our Lord, and his Jesuit spirit with us during his years of ministry here at Christ the King. We are all grateful that Fr. Gino will continue to serve in our locale at St. Joseph Hospital. ♛

Wednesday, July 31, is the feast of St. Ignatius of Loyola, the founder of the Jesuit Order. The Jesuits were founded in the post-reformation era in order to help the Church respond to some of the problems that had triggered the need for reform. The Jesuits are particularly dedicated to education, spiritual direction, and serving wherever there is a need in the Church. I have been on retreats at Jesuit Retreat Centers (including a 30-day retreat 35 years ago), subscribe to a Jesuit magazine, AMERICA, and have been appreciative and personally touched by the ministry of Jesuit priests in our diocese, in Lexington, and here at Christ the King. I am not able to name all the Jesuit priests who have served here but as I name a few, hopefully that will spark your memories of Jesuit priests who have aided you on your spiritual journey.

Many of us fondly remember Father Bob Murphy. We invoke his prayers at the beginning of every Oktoberfest to provide good weather; we see his picture on the wall in Room A of our Parish Life Center. He was a pioneer within our diocese in the implementation of the RCIA process. He lived for 80 years. 20 of those years he served at Christ the King. He helped many people with annulments and guided many who had become inactive to return to the practice of the faith. He loved Christ the King; and the parishioners loved him. His room was on the first floor of the O'Neill Center when it served as both residence and office. His room was the present-day "living room"; so it was close to the receptionist's desk; in fact, on many days he would welcome people and answer the phone during the receptionist's lunch hour. In his later years, when the priests lived in a condo on Duke Road, he had a lift chair taking him to his upstairs apartment and he and his guardian angel would ride a scooter between the condo and church.

I remember Father Lou Lipps who lived here for many years, while serving as a spiritual director who traveled throughout Eastern Kentucky to guide many people's spiritual journeys. He had a special care for the poor who lived in Lexington's inner-city and he enjoyed his status as a Santa Claus look-alike. One of the highlights of his life was ministering to pilgrims at Lourdes, dividing his time between hearing confessions and helping the handicapped into the healing waters. For many years, he was my spiritual director, with whom I met monthly. For years Father Hank Kenny had a room in our office where he saw folks to whom he was providing spiritual direction and counseling and he offered daily Mass at noon here for many years. Many around the community still recall the kind pastoral spirit of Father George Maynard, who was a V.A. chaplain for years.

Over the recent years so many of us have been blessed by the ministry of Father Gino, with his energy, creativity, joy and wisdom. We are grateful for his continual ministry in our community in many different ways as he continues to love and serve. On Saturday, August 24, when we have a Senior's Seminar, he will offer the 8 a.m. Mass and guide a session on Spirituality and Aging. Living with Father Gino is Father Bob Bueter, who helped Lexington Catholic grow beyond many people's dreams as Father Walt Bado, who served for years at U.K.'s Newman Center and who continues to touch many people's lives by his gentle wisdom and goodness.

And of course, any reflection on the impact of Jesuits has to include our current Pope Francis, who lives out and shares the Jesuit spirit and vision with the world. This week particularly, I encourage you to express your gratitude to those Jesuits who have blessed you by their gifts and to lift them up in prayer. ♛

# CHAPTER 25

*Diversity Within Unity:*

BULLETIN — September 24, 2017

BULLETIN — September 9, 2018

BULLETIN — August 18, 2019

BULLETIN — April 11, 2021

This Thursday, September 28 at 6:30 p.m. in our School Library, I will offer an Evening of Discussion on Inter-faith Marriages. All are invited. I am aware that a number of our families with children in our school and CCD programs are families where only one parent is Catholic. Many of the weddings celebrated in Catholic Churches in Lexington are interfaith weddings. When Catholicism is a low percentage of the population, as it is in Eastern and Central Kentucky, interfaith friendships, and eventually interfaith marriages are a logical outcome. At this Thursday's program, I will offer some input and then invite questions and discussion.

Many of us can verify that the "promises" involved in an interfaith marriage preparation have evolved over the years to a position which is more respectful of the dedication that both husband and wife will have to their respective faiths. We see more and more interfaith cooperation in social ministries such as B.U.I.L.D., Bible studies, and our current Catholic-Lutheran program observing the 500th Anniversary of the beginning of the Protestant Reformation. Our youth are often involved in the Fellowship of Christian Athletes and other youth ministry activities which are non-denominational. Catholic hospitals will have chaplains of various religions; many large hospitals will have a Catholic chaplain on the staff. When a loved and respected person is sick, prayers and compassion know no denominational boundaries. One of the joys I have experienced as a priest in our diocese (which I probably would not have had in a diocese where Catholicism is 50 percent of the population) is the set of friendships with local Protestant ministers. Whenever someone is in the RCIA who has been baptized with water in the name of the Trinity, the Catholic Church acknowledges their Baptism, does not call for a second Baptism, and in the Rite of Reception gratefully acknowledges the Christian formation provided by the Protestant Church.

The Jewish, Muslim, and other religions are less prevalent in our area than is Christianity, but we have respect for the religious and spiritual characteristics of all faith traditions.

When we consider the many Churches within Christianity, there is much more we hold in common than there is which divides us. Whether a Protestant Church is a mega-Church, a mainline county-seat Church, or a small rural Church, we all share some basic aspects. Of course there are differences, but too often we focus on the differences more so than our common core of beliefs and practices.

Next Sunday, October 1 at 2 p.m., our Cathedral will host a joint Concert of Lutheran and Catholic singers and musicians. It is striking that Martin Luther realized the spiritual power of singing, advocated for more singing by the congregation during Mass, and wrote many hymns, including the classic "A Mighty Fortress is Our God". I hope you can join us next Sunday afternoon. A reception in Hehman Hall will follow the concert.

Finally, I once again invite you to the Thursday evening program described at the beginning of this article...parents in an interfaith marriage, grandparents, couple planning for marriage...all are invited. On Thursday, our nursery is open, providing child-care. I thank our school administration for co-sponsoring Thursday's program. ♛

Always at our Oktoberfest, we meet some folks from our parish whom we have not seen in a while. Pundits have described the Catholic Church as "here comes everybody." That is part of our story as a Catholic Church. We do have a lot of diversity. It is not enough to say that we are made up of conservatives and liberals, nor to make distinctions based on age, where the children go to school, or the length of time as parishioners.

Father James Bacik, in his book *A Light Unto My Path* offers seven ways to describe Catholics in our present times.

1) **Eclipsed** — They seldom attend Mass or pray. Some of these folks describe themselves as too busy and have other priorities; others feel guilty and unworthy. And yet they identify themselves as Catholic.

2) **Private** — They seldom attend Mass or participate in church activities, but pursue spiritual goals by reading religious books, communing with nature, or praying privately. They do not have a strong appreciation of the value of community or our religious tradition.

3) **Ecumenical** — They feel that the divisions among Christians make no sense, that all churches should unite and work together, and that if any church brings them closer to Jesus and meets their spiritual needs, that is the place to go.

4) **Evangelical** — They place a high value on the importance of a personal relationship with Jesus, belong to prayer groups, exude great energy and enthusiasm, and seek to protect the church from threats from the contemporary world and dangerous teachings within the church.

5) **Sacramental** — Many Catholics love the Church and regularly attend Mass and participate in the other sacraments and other traditional practices of prayer. Often they live with a sense that there is the presence of God in every aspect of life. Sometimes they can evolve into living on a spiritual plateau, with a kind of flatness.

6) **Prophetic** — Within Catholicism some folks have a passion to work for peace and justice, to address the issues in the Church, in one's community, or in the state, nation or world that need to be changed. Involvement in the Church and an understanding of the tradition of the Church's Social teachings are at the heart of this activity. They are often frustrated, and even angry because their parish and the Church in general is not embracing the causes to which they are dedicated.

7) **Communal** — These Catholics seek parishes and small groups of people who share their commitments, who have similar values, and who have kindred spirits and they do not want to dialogue or find common ground with folks who have different priorities. They often have an idealized and insular approach to their community.

Of course, many of us fit more than one of these categories. Yet they offer a picture of who we are as a Church and as a parish. And with the heart of Jesus, we seek to respect one another and realize that there is no one ideal way to be a Catholic Christian. And so the spirit of our Oktoberfest is one of the strongest expressions of our welcome and our readiness to accompany any and all on your journey with the Church and with Jesus. ♔

W hen I go on retreat, I almost always enter into the prayer, "Lord I believe, help my unbelief..." I do believe, but I realize that there can be more consistency, more intensity, more clarity, more dedication. And yet, the biggest reason why I am a priest is because of the importance of the search for God and seeking to live with God at the center of life...this is a quest we all share and I am at peace with my life-long call to walk with fellow believers and searchers. Daily prayer, the Divine Office, Mass, meeting monthly with a priests' prayer group, meeting monthly with a spiritual director, and an annual retreat are all part of the ways I am able to keep in touch with Jesus and to keep the spiritual fires burning.

And yet, one more way I continue to experience Jesus and his call and his love is through the example, the encouragement and the prayers of the people I serve and with whom I walk...I mean you!

I thank you for your faith, your hope and your love as these virtues extend to your family and friends, to the church and our parish, to our community and to our world, to the poor and those who are often forgotten.

This is a weekend when we are focusing on stewardship. Stewardship is not just a Church catchword which we annually acknowledge, check off our list, and move on. Stewardship is not just a focus on financial giving. Stewardship is another way to describe discipleship, or life as a vibrant parish-member.

Vibrant parish members are grateful for the blessings they have received and will receive from the Lord through the life of their parish, and so they give of themselves to the community. Vibrant parish members give of their time, their talent and their financial resources, and in so doing, they receive deeper blessings as they encounter Jesus and his people through their investment.

One way to understand stewardship is through the ministry of Habitat for Humanity volunteers...they join with the family who is in need and together they build a house which becomes a family home. It is a faith-based effort, and becomes a labor of love and an expression of community. There is a deep joy as the volunteers work together, culminated in the day when the new home is dedicated and blessed.

We are living in a challenging and exciting time in our parish's history. We are involved in our major campaign to rehab our parish home, our church and our school, to make it safer, more secure, and more efficient. We need to find a way to do one more surge in our campaign of giving, of generosity, of seeing and fulfilling the vision. Even more so, we realize that our collective faith can go deeper. We have many parishioners who are not as active as they once were. We all need to work and pray together as we seek to rehabilitate our community's faith and dedication to the Catholic way of life.

I am grateful for the ministry of the Catholic Stewardship Consultants, who have guided this weekend's retreat and to Deacon Larry Cranfill, of St. Mildred's in Somerset, as he joins us this weekend and preaches at our Masses on Stewardship, Discipleship and Evangelization. ♛

A wonderful five-point code for a person seeking to live holy life is to have a dedication to one's faith and acknowledge God's supremacy, to pray daily (in fact, five times daily) to regularly give alms to the poor, to fast and seek God's mercy, and to make a pilgrimage to a holy place.

This list comprises the Five Pillars of Islam. This Tuesday begins the Islamic month of Ramadan, where Muslims fast every day from food and drink during the daylight hours. If you have ever been to Jerusalem or any other community where there are minarets, you will hear the haunting chant calling people to prayer and fasting. Ramadan is a season of reflection, repentance and purification, trusting the mercy of Allah. At the Good Friday liturgy, we pray in a special way for our fellow monotheists who honor Abraham as one of their spiritual fathers. And we are grateful for the way that the Islamic religion guides many people to live saintly lives.

Throughout the world of religion and spirituality, a core principle is that God is merciful. The 12 steps of Alcoholics Anonymous begins with the realization that only God can free a person from the power of an addiction and that, however the Supreme Being is understood, God desires to have mercy.

Mercy is different than sympathy or compassion. Mercy is related to power...We have the power to extend mercy, to express our belief that another person is more than their worst action, that God is still stirring within them, that they are not hopeless.

Today, we celebrate Divine Mercy Sunday. We focus in a special way on the Divine Mercy extended by Jesus as lived on earth and as he continues to abide with us. We trust the mercy of Jesus which continues to bless us particularly through the sacraments of Eucharist and Penance.

One of the hallmarks of Pope Francis is his emphasis on the mercy of God and the importance of the Church and its members to be agents of mercy.

We have been praying for the mercy of God throughout the pandemic. We pray for mercy for those who have been seriously ill during this time. We have been challenged to personally have a spirit of mercy towards those who have acted in a hurtful and violent manner during these trying times. In many of our families, we are called to have a spirit of mercy towards those who disappoint us and are alienated. We need to have mercy towards those whose hearts have been broken by the terrible experiences they have had and their attendant grief. Life can be hard. Our Gracious and Mysterious God gives room for our world and our lives to be chaotic and unfair. Occasionally in our darkest times, we need to have mercy on God and trust that God is greater than our idea or experience of God.

Life is full of "both-ands" more so than "either-ors". We can be both merciful and realistic; our love can be both forgiving and tough. Let us pray that as we imperfect human beings continue our own journeys through life, that we will draw from the example and the teaching of Jesus who is both merciful and just. ♛

# CHAPTER 26

## *Jesus:*

This weekend we celebrate the *Feast of Christ the King*. It serves as an occasion to celebrate the joy we have when we center our lives on Jesus, when fidelity to the way of Jesus is the guiding principle of our lives, when our relationship with Jesus defines our lives. We are continually growing in faith, still yearning for the personal experience of Jesus, still hoping to feel the presence of Jesus in such a powerful way that our lives are changed.

And so we stay with our daily prayers; we read the scriptures and pray the gospels; we reverently sit in the presence of the Blessed Sacrament; we find encouragement in the lives of the saints. We work at connecting with Jesus. Yet, much of our most important work is to get the clutter out of the way so that we can open the doors of our hearts when Jesus calls our name.

The *Feast of Christ the King* concludes the church year. It is a fitting end as we acknowledge the mighty power of our Redeemer King. Next weekend when we begin the 4 week season of Advent, we prepare to welcome the Infant King who was born as a baby with the vulnerability which is part of the human condition.

In this Sunday's Gospel, Jesus describes the works of mercy which are done consciously and unconsciously as we live in the light of Christ Our King. This is a good time for all of us to be grateful for the people who have touched our lives and blessed us over the years by the ways they have cared for us in our vulnerable times...and it is a good time to recall that our charity at this time of the year opens our hearts to go deeper as people who share the merciful spirit of Jesus with those who are in need...and in so doing, we are further united with Jesus.

The *Feast of Christ the King* is also our parish feast day. Our parish was founded in the immediate aftermath of World War II. It was founded at a time when totalitarian

dictators had tried to render Jesus irrelevant. As the present-day faith community of Christ the King, we can declare by word and by deed how important Jesus is. He is Our King. Jesus on the cross is our King. Jesus in the manger is our King. Jesus healing the sick is our King. Jesus teaching his apostles is our King. Jesus on that first Easter morning is our King. Jesus in the Eucharist is our King. We can declare this by our words, but we make a much more powerful statement when we center our lives on Jesus. The Good News is that Jesus is our King. In the words of Pope Francis...that is the "Joy of the Gospel". ⛪

It is one of the most challenging questions we face. "Who do you say Jesus is?" Jesus asked the question of his disciples. It continues to be an important question. On this feast of Christ the King, I will offer a few thoughts on my perception of Jesus. I offer these as stimuli for your own reflection and answer to the question.

Jesus is a teacher. He taught a new way of living. He taught the way of love, of the desire to know God's will, the way of non-violence, the way of humility. Jesus was a man of prayer, he began his ministry after a retreat in the desert, and frequently took time away from ministry to go to the other side of the Sea of Galilee for quiet time. Jesus was a rabbi, a man of the Jewish religion, who built upon the Jewish religion and heritage. To a great extent, his prayer book was the Old Testament.

*Photo by Maureen Guarnieri-Yeager*

As a teacher, Jesus was also a mentor and team-builder, as he developed twelve disciples into apostles who would move beyond his own geographic territory and begin the process of establishing the New Way of the Gospel. Jesus was inclusive. He reached out to Jew and Gentile, to rich and poor, to men and women, to the virtuous and to sinners. His teachings were often met by rejection, and his teachings led many to seek to discredit or obliterate him.

Jesus was a healer. Jesus healed the sick, he drove the evil spirits out of people who were possessed, he healed those who were living without hope or dignity, and he raised the dead to life and restored vitality to those worn down by life's cares. Jesus taught that sins can be forgiven. He shared with his first priests his power of healing, of reconciling, and of consecrating.

Jesus was a friend — and he still is. He was a friend to Lazarus, Martha, Mary, Mary Magdalene; he certainly had a deep affection for his disciples; children and sinners, and untouchables — such as Samaritans and the lepers — found Jesus to be a friend. Jesus is still with us as a friend whom we meet in our daily prayers, at times of crises, and in our Eucharist.

Jesus is our Redeemer. He gave his life for us. He showed us that the way of truth and integrity will free others. He died on the cross for our sins. He came to serve, not to be served. He taught us by his example of foot-washing. And he is a hero. He taught us from the cross to continue in prayer, to pray with honesty, to trust the power of forgiveness, to seek to do the will of God.

Jesus is God. He rose from the dead. He gave us his Holy Spirit to convey wonderful spiritual gifts. Jesus transcends history. He is with us in every Holy Communion, in every Baptism, Confirmation and, Confession, in every tabernacle, but also in every moment in our lives when we see Him with the eyes of faith. And yet he had a human nature. He began his human life as a baby and wept, laughed, hurt, and loved good meals..."God so loved the world, that He sent his only begotten Son."

Jesus is not a problem to solve, but a Mystery to encounter and allow to reveal more and more who we can be. ◼

Today we begin the holiest of all weeks. In John's Gospel, when the Holy Thursday Passover Meal and the foot-washing are finished, Jesus gives a teaching to his disciples and us. It is called the Great Discourse; it comprises the four chapters which lead into John's presentation of the Passion and Death of Jesus. It is the culmination of the teachings of Jesus, offering a message of encouragement to those who will follow him in preaching the Good News. The very first words of this message are the beginning of chapter 14, "Do not let your hearts be troubled. Have faith in God and faith in me." As you and I have our own ways of the cross and as we face our own challenges in walking with Jesus, these words offer wisdom and hope. Jesus is with us...let us pray that our observance of this Holy Week will open our eyes and hearts even more so to the abiding presence of Jesus, and the fervent desire that Jesus has that we live the fullness of life.

In the Great Discourse of Jesus, another highlight is in John 15:13. "There is no greater love than this, to lay down one's life for one's friends." Jesus assures us that we are his friends and that he is ready to give his life for us. It is awesome; the great love of Jesus inspires awe and wonder, and boggles the mind. God comes into the world and as Jesus lays down his life, faces rejection and abandonment by his followers, and endures horrific suffering and a humiliating death Jesus redeems you and me. As the hymn goes... "What wondrous love is this, oh, my soul...oh, my soul".

*Photo by Maureen Guarnieri-Yeager*

It is a great expression of love to lay down our lives for those we love. We see this sacrifice in family life, as husbands and wives decide against career upward-mobility so that there can be more focus on care for their children and aging parents. We see this as parents forego some of their personal dreams so that their children can receive the education that will prepare them to be Christian leaders. We see this laying down of one's agenda as the heart of conflict resolution and efforts of forgiveness because listening and letting go of past hurts are essential — difficult as it is. We see this spirit of joyful sacrifice in those who donate one of their kidneys so that another person can live a fruitful life. We see this daily in our parish, as so many of you give your time as volunteers, offer your skills, and financially support the mission of our Church and the stabilizing of our cathedral structures. We see this gift of time as so many of you come to our Adoration Chapel and open yours minds, hearts and souls to the counter-cultural silence from which Jesus occasionally speaks.

It is striking that Jesus speaks of laying down his life in the context of the Institution of the Eucharist. Jesus loves us so much that he gives himself to us in the humble hosts we consecrate at Mass. "What wondrous love is this..." Jesus so desires to help us to live good lives, Jesus is so ready to redeem us, Jesus lays down his life for us, Jesus gives himself to us in order to nourish us for the challenges of life. ♛

This week, on Tuesday, we celebrate the feast of the Transfiguration of Jesus. The Transfiguration is the fourth of the Luminous Mysteries of the Rosary. It is recorded in the Gospels of Mark, Matthew and Luke. It is always the Gospel reading for the Second Sunday of Lent.

The Transfiguration describes the time when Jesus went onto a mountain in Galilee to pray. He was accompanied by Peter, James and John. As Jesus prayed, his appearance was changed before their eyes. Jesus became radiant; in effect, his holiness and Godliness shone through in a way that could not be questioned. Moses and Elijah appeared and Jesus seemed to be in conversation with them. In effect, Jesus was manifested as the one fulfilling the inter-connection of the law and the Exodus journey to freedom and the importance of the prophetic spirit and the message of those inspired by God's Spirit to offer hope and challenge.

Peter speaks for many of us as he wants to build some tents and stay in the experience of glory for as long as possible. Jesus however knows that now is the time to move on, to go down the mountain, and in fact, to begin the journey south to Jerusalem. Jesus was fairly well received in the area of Galilee where the religious and political establishments were not as deeply defining the culture as they were in Jerusalem.

In many ways, the event of the Transfiguration was a gift to the apostles and to those with whom they shared their account of the episode. In Jerusalem Jesus would give the Supreme Witness to the power of the Good News as he faced rejection, denial betrayal, a travesty of a trial, imprisonment, torture and death on the cross. The Transfiguration strengthened the resolve of Jesus, but it also strengthened the faith of the disciples as they eventually responded with heroic faith to the resurrection and the bestowal of the Holy Spirit and the attendant gifts.

Truly the Transfiguration was a Luminous event, giving a clear and radiant presentation of the divinity of Jesus. As you and I live our lives, we have had and will have our own luminous events. They will not reveal our divinity of course, but they will remind us that we are temples of the Holy Spirit, that we have done some things which have made life better for some people, and that we have the capacity to make a difference in our world, whether on a micro or macro level.

Too often as we live our lives and as we pray, we focus on our sins, faults, the evil, destructive and foolish things we have done. Most of us have the ability to balance this list of flaws and faults with the good decisions we have made, the occasions when we have lived and given with Christ-like charity, and the occasions when we have mysteriously been in the right place at the right time and have done or said something that was graceful beyond our personal limitations...These are "transfiguration moments."

They are not just occasions for putting a trophy on a shelf, but they are illuminations of what we are capable of and who we are when we allow the Lord's Spirit to guide us. ♛

Here at Christ the King we observed the Vigil of Ash Wednesday not by a Mardi Gras party, but by a prayer service focused on the Holy Face of Jesus. It is a common yearning among Christians to envision the Face of Jesus, to have a sense of the reality of the Incarnate God, and to move forward in our quest for an intimate relationship with Jesus.

Many people are moved by the face of Jesus imprinted within the Shroud of Turin; many others appreciate the Shroud's image as a helpful clue in their search to experience the face of Jesus. One of the meditations on a Cursillo weekend retreat is entitled the "Glance of Christ" and it centers on Jesus seeing Peter in the garden after Peter had denied Jesus. This glance of Jesus saw into the depths of Peter's soul, led Peter to face the truth of his inconsistency and fear, and offered forgiveness to Peter. In the same way Jesus sees into who we are with our flaws and sins and yet offers forgiveness and empowerment. The priest who gave that meditation when I was a participant on my first Cursillo was Fr. Charles McDonald. He very dramatically held up a large mirror and said to all of us retreatants as he walked around the room, flashing the mirror in front of each of us..."Here is the Face of Christ." In a way he was right...when we become fully Christian, we reflect Christ. The quest need not go to exotic and esoteric lengths. St. Irenaeus has famously written, "The glory of God is someone fully alive." And yet human nature leads us to search for the key which will take us to a deeper relationship with and a deeper faith in Jesus.

When I was a campus minister at Eastern Kentucky University, I asked one of the students, who majored in art, to make a portrait of a man whose face was a composite of Jesus and my own father. My father died when I was six. I knew he had blessed me with his fatherly love, but I did not have many clear memories of him. This portrait was an effort to connect with two good men whom I did not know very well...When I was on sabbatical for three months in San Francisco, one of my first personally imposed agenda items was to page through a book of classic portraits of Jesus till I found the one that spoke to me. Then I printed a copy of, framed and hung in my room the face of "Jesus the Healer."

Moses heard God say, "No one can see the face of God and live." And yet Moses talked with God face to face numerous times. Perhaps the meaning of the statement is that no one can see the face of God and continue to live as they have been living, that no one can see the face of God and not die to their false self and be reborn as their true self.

On this the first Lenten Sunday, we reflect on the face of Jesus as he prayed in the desert, as he faced the temptations from the evil spirit and as he emerged from the desert retreat, prepared to begin his ministry. Next week, the Gospel will present the episode of Jesus being transfigured and his face shining in glory. When we arrive at Holy Week, we will envision the face of Jesus at the Last Supper, on Good Friday and on Easter as he began to make a series of appearances to his disciples.

And yet, we are also called to trust the mystery, to be content with seeing and not seeing as clearly as we would like to. That is part of the Great Mystery of the Real Presence of Jesus in the Blessed Sacrament. Jesus is with us, Body and Blood; we may not see his face in a way that is universally acknowledged, but our Mysterious God who lavishly loves us, continues to reveal layer after layer of the Divine Being. ♛

# CHAPTER 27

*Confession:*

BULLETIN — July 31, 2016

BULLETIN — February 18, 2018

BULLETIN — April 7, 2019

BULLETIN — March 7, 2021

Here at Christ the King, the Sacrament of Reconciliation is a key component of our ministry during a typical week. We have many different occasions when the priests are available for this sacrament of healing and we have many people who take advantage of the opportunities we offer.

Throughout the Church three key words describe what happens with this sacrament.

We go to confession. After prayer, examining our conscience and admitting our need and desire to change our lives, we tell our sins to a priest. Very often spiritual direction is included in this dialogue. This is confession.

We call it the Sacrament of Penance. We are sorry (penitential) and, after we confess our sins, the priest suggests a penance, and we pledge to do special prayers, works of mercy, or some other spiritual practice to remind ourselves of the need to work on our lives and the need to re-direct our lives away from sin.

Most correctly, it is the Sacrament of Reconciliation as we are re-united with the Church, the Lord and our principles and we are pointed towards reconciliation with those we have hurt and with our true selves.

Very often a priest/confessor is called a Doctor of the Soul. This week the Church presents three feasts of outstanding Doctors of the Soul.

On Thursday we celebrate the feast of St. John Vianney, the Curé of Ars (1785-1859). He was a simple and yet holy and brilliantly insightful priest who was a country pastor in the obscure French village of Ars. His ability to see the issues beneath what was being confessed, his compassion, and his prayerful exemplification of love for Jesus drew such crowds that he heard confessions for hours at a time and the local railroad made a special re-routing to bring people to Ars so that they could receive the Sacrament of reconciliation from him. St. John Vianney is the patron saint of parish priests.

Monday is the feast of St. Alphonsus Ligouri, who lived from 1696 till 1787. He was a scholar and prolific write who was also a very important moral theologian whose teachings have helped penitents and confessors find the balance between rigid legalism and laxity as they examined their consciences and considered flawed human nature and the reality of sin.

This Sunday, July 31 is the feast day of St. Ignatius Loyola (1491-1556). St. Ignatius is the founder of the Jesuits, the developer of the famous Spiritual Exercises, and the inspiration for the practice of much of contemporary spiritual direction. Through the influence of St. Ignatius many people have been guided to make good decisions, to live virtuous lives, and to feel the presence of the lord.

Particularly on this feast day (understated because it falls on a Sunday) we give thanks for the ministry of Fr. Gino and his fellow Jesuits in Lexington, Frs. Walt Bado, Bob Bueter, and George Von Kaenel. 👑

> 66 *Particularly on this feast day (understated because it falls on a Sunday) we give thanks for the ministry of Fr. Gino and his fellow Jesuits in Lexington, Frs. Walt Bado, Bob Bueter, and George Von Kaenel.* 99

The Greek philosopher Socrates is frequently quoted as he stated that "The unexamined life is not worth living." In that light I offer a few comments on upcoming events.

As we began Lent, most of us have prayerfully examined our lives and have seen a need for further growth and based on that examination, we have made resolutions to make some changes.

This Monday at 7:30 p.m. we will have our Parish Penance Service for the season of Lent. Bishop John and six other priests will be available for confessions following a short prayer service to dispose us for the reception of this wonderful sacrament of spiritual cleansing and strengthening. Always an important element of the Sacrament of Penance is the Examination of Conscience, and to look at our individual lives to determine what we need to confess, what sins we need to be healed of, and what attitudes need to be changed. The examination of conscience also includes a reflection on our blessings and our strengths.

Most of the time at a Penance Service there is a list of actions and attitudes that prompts penitents to examine their lives and to name their sins. A solid examination of conscience reflects on the 10 commandments and the laws of the Church. In addition to what sins we have committed, it is helpful to examine our attitudes. The basis for this is often the Seven Capital Sins, attitudes which put us on the slippery slope leading to sin. The Seven Capital Sins are pride, gluttony, lust, anger, jealousy, envy and sloth. The Examined Life is a key to a healthy spiritual life, to continued growth as a disciple, and to the cultivation of the virtue of integrity.

During the third, fourth, and fifth Sundays of Lent, there is the Rite of the Scrutinies at a Mass each weekend. This examination is for the catechumens who are preparing for Baptism, Confirmation and Communion at the Easter Vigil. They are questioned regarding their readiness to be vibrant Catholic Christian disciples. Yet as the people in the assembly at those Masses have the opportunity to examine ourselves and to affirm that we too are ready for the next step to which Jesus is calling us. Lent is a time of retreat; it is a time of getting ready for the next steps in our spiritual pilgrimages. The self-examination which is at the heart of the scrutinies is a key part of that process.

Our Capital Campaign is related to the thorough examination of our building which Joe Sandfort, our Facilities Manager, has guided us through. We are preparing ourselves for the future as we respond to the many needs of our aging building...thanks to all who have examined your financial resources and have stepped forward to help support our repairs and rehabilitation.

Many parishioners have had favorable comments about our pre-Mass review of the essential elements of the Mass. It is good for all of us to examine our attitude and focus as we gather for prayer at the Eucharistic source and summit of our lives.

In many ways the journey of life is one examination after another. May we see what we need to see as we examine our lives and the movement of God's Spirit within. ♛

D uring the season of Lent, many of us go to confession. We receive the grace of this Sacrament of Reconciliation. We examine our consciences, realize the hurtfulness of our sins, pray with sorrow, and ask for God's grace to help us to change our lives. We do penance in order to help ourselves to move in the right direction. And we confess to a priest. Sometimes the confession is at a scheduled time before one of our Masses or at a prayer service which includes confessions. Sometimes we set an appointment and talk in depth with a priest. Sometimes we go face-to-face; sometimes we speak anonymously. Sometimes there is a particular intensity, as we hope that the confession and the absolution of this sacrament will help us to work through an addiction, compulsion or bad habit.

And sometimes, we come when we have not received the sacrament for a long time. It might even be years. But something is stirring; very often God's spirit is Stirring...and we know that this Lent is the time, we feel like we need to do it before Easter.

In the monthly booklet, *Give Us This Day*, there is a meditation entitled, "Prayer before Confession after a Long Absence".

*I confess Lord, it's been a while...And I am ashamed...*
*My guilt just seemed to get in the way...and now I've put this off for too long...*
*Why did I let myself stay so far away from you...*
*when I know in my heart that You have never left?...*
*I am afraid, Lord, that if I reveal myself to you...show you who I have become...*
*that you will not recognize me as your own...*
*So I beg, look upon me as you would look upon your Son, Jesus, that you might see and*
*love in me what you see and love in Christ.*
*Then when I rise and go to you...I shall be overwhelmed with love...*
*when you come running to me with your arms wide open. Amen*
— DIANA MACALINTAL, *The Work of Your Hands* 👑

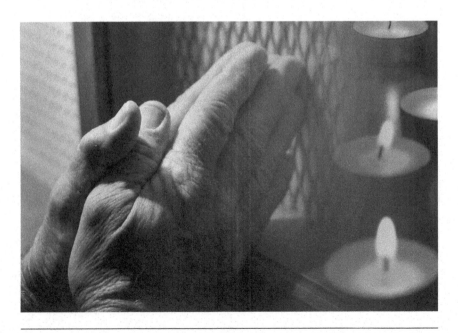

L ast weekend we had several pamphlets on the table by the Hehman Hall entry to Church. They were "free for the taking." By far, the most popular one was the pamphlet entitled, "Getting more out of Confession."

I have noticed that the pandemic-related need to adjust our lifestyles and to spend more time in a quiet, somewhat isolated manner has led many of us to undertake a review of our life. We do this intentionally, and sometimes the memories of our mistakes, foolishness and sins just flood us.

We here at Christ the King have been able to offer the Sacrament of Reconciliation... and it is striking how many people are taking advantage of the opportunities we offer.

It is important to name the resistance to come to confession. There is embarrassment at our sins and sometimes a feeling of being so stuck in a sinful habit, attitude or action that the idea of changing one's life feels hopeless. There is confusion regarding what is sin when there is the sense that "everybody's doing it" or the sin is simply part of imperfect human nature, and therefore not a sin. Some people are reluctant to go to confession because of a prior bad experience in the confessional or because they have a mistrust of priests. Sometimes a person is locked in a hardness of heart because of an injustice or hurt done to them or to a loved one and does not feel ready to move towards forgiving or being reconciled. And sometimes the resistance is fairly basic...the person does not know how to go to confession as an adult or does not believe in the power of the sacrament. I am sure there are more reasons for resisting the use of this Sacrament.

It is even more important to list why so many people do make the choice to go to confession. The sacrament guarantees forgiveness from God and the Church; even if the person's sorrow is "imperfect", there is still forgiveness. The grace of the Sacrament helps us to change our lives, helps us to forgive ourselves (often one of the greatest challenges of our spiritual lives!), and helps us to be open to and begin a process of forgiving those whom we have a difficult time forgiving...or at least praying for them, wanting their improvement, and noticing any steps forward. Confession helps us to be honest with ourselves and with another. Confession is good for the soul, it is cathartic. From a holistic standpoint, confession and its unburdening also relieves stress and its attendant ailments. Most priests listen with a trained and dedicated intensity and offer acceptance, compassion, hope, counseling, appropriate challenge and spiritual direction. Confession is an expression of faith, and very often there is a sense of the presence of Jesus in the confessional encounter.

It is best to see the Sacrament of Penance as a gift more so than an imposition. I often think of the little boy who made his first confession and talked through some problems he was having with his brother. He could sense that the priest understood and that his sin was forgivable and that he could do better and he was ready to try harder. As he was leaving Church, someone asked him how it went. His face lit up, he gave a kind of cheer with his hands and arms and said, "I feel great!" ▄

# CHAPTER 28

*Labor Day:*

BULLETIN — September 3, 2017

BULLETIN — September 6, 2020

We celebrate Labor Day weekend and give thanks for the blessings of our work. Many of us can look back on our youth and the first jobs we had which provided a paycheck...and which also taught us the importance of responsibility. We learned a lot from those experiences. Many of us also remember the dedication we saw in our parents as they worked and often sacrificed so that we could live good lives.

When we finished our schooling, many of us entered our first jobs that served as our occupations. We notice the hand of God in action as many times we were moved or transferred to a position outside our initial interests, and then something inside us caught fire.

We also know the reality that many of us do work which is not very stimulating, but, in order to live well and to support our families, we stay with the day by day challenge.

Many of us socialize with the people with whom we work. Some of our best friends are co-workers. We talk about religion, families, life and death with them. The workplace is very often the place where divisions based on race, sex or beliefs are diminished. It is a wonderful feeling when a project at work is addressed successfully by a team. The commitment to quality production at work spills into every other aspect of life.

It is important to celebrate the breakthroughs in employment practices, hiring, benefits, wages, insurance, sick leave and other legal issues which lead to fair and wholesome work environments. We give thanks for superiors who know how to teach, lead, confront and express appreciation. We pray for the gifts of wisdom and courage for all those who work in situations of stress and emotional debilitation. We encourage those who need to leap into the dark as they leave a job that is soul-draining. We give thanks for those who lead from the top, from the center or from the grass roots in calling for ethical work practices. We who work for and within the Church have a special responsibility to be a light reflecting the joy of a grace-filled work environment

We give thanks for all the parents who work from home or whose work is day-by-day house-keeping and family care. There is much dignity in that commitment and its attendant sacrifices. We also give thanks for the many volunteers who apply their work-skills and work-ethic to the quest to make the world a better place.

We pray for all who are unemployed. We realize that Eastern Kentucky particularly is plagued by a gross lack of jobs. We pray for refugees and immigrants whose first step towards normalization is a regular decent job. We pray for the disabled who are unable to work and who question their self-worth. We pray for the work-a-holics we know and those who drive themselves and their subordinates too hard. Everyone needs balance.

And finally, we give thanks for those who are retired, who rejoice that one season is over, but another season is upon them, a season which is very often a passage into deeper spirituality. ◾

Labor Day is a day to give thanks for the blessing of work and to give thanks for the workers who make our world a better place. Our thoughts, reflections and prayers certainly go in a unique direction as we commemorate Labor Day in this year of the pandemic.

Many people are working almost exclusively from home. This approach has the purpose of keeping them and others safe. Many workers miss the comradery of being with fellow workers. Many parents who have been working at home also need to care for their children who are taking virtual classes. And so, there needs to be much more involvement in the educational process, even while doing one's job. One of the challenges has been to manage time and to know when the working day begins and ends. The side benefits, however, include more family time, more involvement in their children's education, including religious formation, and the expanding realization of the possibilities of communication and learning through the use of technology.

This Labor Day we hold in our hearts those who have lost their jobs in the midst of the pandemic and those who own businesses which have had to close or radically curtail their activity and their workforce. It is stressful to face the uncertainty of how much longer one's job will last. We are grateful for the variety of government grants and charitable contributions which have helped many people and businesses. We face the challenge of unemployment and are grateful to see a rising spirit of charity.

This Labor Day we are grateful for those who have risen to the occasion. Businesses of all sorts have developed their "safe at work" protocol for staff and customers. Factories have restructured their assembly lines to produce personal protection equipment and ventilators. Many companies have worked diligently to find ways to create social distancing and sanitization procedures for workers. We are grateful for the dedication of health care workers and first responders who are serving generously and face the drain of personal grief and their own physical vulnerability. A new job has emerged — contact tracers. We are grateful for the leadership of our elected officials who are guiding us through a situation they would never have imagined as they ran for office. Meanwhile, we pray and hope for the success of the researchers who are vigorously working to develop a vaccine.

This Labor Day we face the reality of racial disparity in the job market as we own the racism that is still prevalent within our culture and, at least subtly in many of us. And we face our national ambivalence in welcoming immigrants who simply want to live in peace and are willing to do the work that no one else wants to do. We are all horrified by instances of violence and mob destruction and we seek to balance respect for police and the stresses they face with the images of brutal excess we have seen too often on the news. And in many ways, professional athletes, whose job is to play games to entertain us, are among the prophetic leaders.

On this Labor Day I am grateful for and proud of the many ways every member of our parish's pastoral staff have risen to the occasion, made creative adaptations to their ministry, and have been of support to one another and to me. I am grateful for and proud of all the faculty members of our school for the way they prepared through the summer for the reopening of our school. I am grateful for the many contractors and their staff members who have been working on our parish capital campaign and reopening projects through the summer. And I am grateful for the many volunteers within our parish who have emerged who have helped us to reopen our liturgies and provide a healthy approach to parish activities.

As our governor says, "We will get through this together."...with the assistance and guidance of God's Holy Spirit. Meanwhile...let's continue to WORK at staying safe and keeping others safe. ♛

# CHAPTER 29

*The Eucharist:*

The *Feast of Corpus Christi* is the feast of the Body and Blood of Christ. This feast day is punctuated by an outdoor procession with Jesus present in the Eucharist being reverently carried throughout our neighborhood as an expression of our faith and our mission. Our neighbors who have mixed emotions about our Oktoberfest and who enjoy our playground have the added opportunity to be touched by the Body of Christ processing and the Body of Christ being processed around the block which comprises our Cathedral land. I thank our liturgical committee, the Knights of Columbus, and all others who have helped in the preparations for this celebration.

The Feast of Corpus Christi invites us to reflect of the Real Presence of Jesus in the Eucharist and the power of Holy Communion. Many people throughout our community are touched by their time of prayer and reflection in our Adoration Chapel. It is wonderful that people can come 24/7 and spend quiet time in the presence of Our Lord. Thanks to all who are members of that committee and those who do the scheduling, and especially to those who come at hours which are most difficult to fill.

Holy Communion is very important. Families celebrate in a major way the First communion of the small children. We are always grateful for the ways catechists and parents teach our children about the Eucharist and prepare them for their First Holy Communion. Many people who become members of the Catholic Church in their adulthood are drawn by our theology and spirituality regarding Holy Communion.

One of the greatest aches in the world of ecumenical relationships is the Catholic teaching that Holy Communion is an expression of union with the Catholic Church and therefore our teaching does not encourage interfaith reception of Holy Communion. This is a delicate issue; many Church leaders and scholars maintain that the ache engendered by this teaching is a motivator to keep working towards Christian unity. Many Catholics who have been inactive for some time return to the Church because of their desire for Holy Communion.

We are very grateful for the ministry of our extraordinary ministers of Communion as they assist at our Masses and also bring Communion to the homebound, hospitalized, and those in nursing homes. In ancient times, Church ministers who offered Communion to the sick and suffering would touch an afflicted person's body with the Body of Christ before giving Communion. We are grateful to Tina Troiano and Rosemary Miller for their coordination of extraordinary ministers at Mass and for the sick respectively.

*Corpus Christi*
**+ P R O C E S S I O N +**

Always at Mass, the bread and wine are transubstantiated into the Body and Blood of Jesus. As we gather as a community of faith and as a Eucharistic people, my prayer is that we all become more and more transformed into living as the Body of Christ. ♛

Here we are on Super Bowl Sunday. Many of us will be at Super Bowl parties, rooting for our favorite team, being with friends and family, enjoying some great snacks, anticipating the over-the-top commercials, wondering what the half-time program will be like, and also analyzing the game.

And yet every Sunday is a Super Sunday for those of us who regularly gather for our Sunday Mass. This Sunday is the Fifth Sunday in Ordinary Time. However, the time is not ordinary. At every Mass this weekend, Jesus becomes present on our altar, in our midst, and in our lives as we celebrate Eucharist and as we receive Him into our lives in Holy Communion.

Our encounter with Jesus at Mass is the high point or summit of our efforts to live as a disciple, as we pray and seek to live day by day as a disciple of Jesus. As we receive Jesus into our lives, He becomes the Source of our efforts to live and share our lives with joy and in a way that generates new life.

Many of us prepare for Mass before we enter the doors of Church. We think and pray about the needs of our family, our world, our Church and ourselves. Many prepare by reading and pondering the scripture readings ahead of time. Families often need to scramble to get everyone moving. It is always good to be greeted and to see some friends and familiar faces as we arrive. We settle in and we open ourselves to what Jesus has to say to us today.

We listen to God's Word, scriptures written at the inspiration of the Holy Spirit. These are messages which spoke to our spiritual ancestors centuries ago and still touch our hearts as the Word of God. We stand for the Gospel because we meet Jesus in the Gospel passage. The first reading generally has a similar theme as that of the Gospel; the second reading makes sure we are touched by the Epistles, written to ancient communities whose issues parallel those of the contemporary Church. Always we sing from a psalm as a response to the readings, a celebration and deepening of a main theme of the Word of God. And we listen as our priest or deacon offers a homily suggesting how God's Word can be a source for our Christ-like living.

Our gifts of bread and wine are then prepared and blessed. There is the beautiful Eucharistic prayer. Jesus comes to us as the Bread of Life. And just as the bread is taken, we recall how God watches over us and yet TAKES us to unexpected and challenging situations in life. Just as the bread is blessed, we recall how our lives continue to be BLESSED. Just as the bread is broken, we acknowledge that a typical life has its experiences of BROKENNESS. And just as the bread has been blessed so that it can be shared...and broken so that it can be shared, we too are called to SHARE from what we have learned through our surviving brokenness and to feel confident in sharing because we trust the blessing of our lives.

The Eucharistic Prayer at the Mass is one of the most beautiful prayers we have. I encourage you to find a way to pray with the words of the Eucharistic Prayer.

Following Communion, we are sent forth on MISSION. We are sent forth to live as disciples. We are sent forth to share the Good News, to personify the Good News. We go forth singing, rejoicing. We have had a peak experience, we have had a Super Sunday — now we are prepared and energized to bring the Light of Jesus into a world too often darkened by sin, fear and insecurity. ♛

This weekend we are concluding our pre-Mass series on the theology and spirituality of the Mass. We are grateful to all those who made presentations and especially to Deacon Tim who designed and directed this project. In essence the program could have been entitled "The Joy of the Eucharist". In this article several key words will be offered as reasons for Eucharistic joy.

ENCOUNTER — We live in a world where God often seems distant, unreachable, and is sometimes regarded as irrelevant or even non-existent. As we struggle with questions of faith, God has given us Jesus and Jesus has given us the Mass as the most regular and reliable way to experience Him. We encounter Jesus in the Gospels, in the prayers of the Mass, and in Holy Communion.

TRANSFORMATION — Many of us have the realization that our lives can be more. We may or may not be plagued with guilt or shame, but we know we can be more. As Jesus comes into our lives, into our souls, the encounter with Jesus permeates our being and takes us closer and closer to living in union with Jesus, living in the spirit of Jesus.

RENEWAL — We live in a world that has many stressors and challenges. It is not easy to live with joy and zest. We struggle with our worries, our failures, and our missed opportunities. We have a difficult time living with a sense of equilibrium. Our weekly Eucharistic celebration reminds us of God's love, of the belief that Jesus has in our worth, and of the continual desire of the Holy Spirit to bless us with gifts which empower us.

UNDERSTANDING — As we stand under the readings, the prayers, the songs, the architectural beauty, the symbolism, the ritual, the blend of the predictable and the unpredictable, we see how much God loves us, how Jesus has given us a great gift, how the Holy Spirit wisely blesses us. We realize that we are far from alone as we travel through life, and that God's words and our worship give a sense of balance to our daily lives. We are guided to understand that true humility is far from powerlessness but is the realization of who we are and the acknowledgement of Who has made us and is watching over us.

TRANSCENDENCE — There is something soothing about the experience of living in a world of mystery, a world that re-affirms that there is more to reality than what meets the eye. The mystery is not some treasure horded by God, but a Gracious and Beautiful Reality which continues to unfold. Every Mass puts us in touch with the Mystery beyond all being who is the Cause and the End of all being.

ENCOURAGEMENT — At Mass, we are with other people...we are with other pilgrims...we are with others who have the same values, the same struggles, the same faith. We pray with and often socialize with one another. We make new friends, we solidify supportive relationships, we give one another courage as we share our stories, and as we share the Great Story of the Good News of Jesus Christ.

MISSION — Every one of us wants to make a difference, and we all can make a difference. As every Mass concludes, we are sent forth to live as vibrant disciples. We can do it. With Jesus and his Spirit inside us, we can have a clarity and confidence as we depart from church and move forward. Having encountered Jesus, having been transformed, renewed and encouraged; having been enlightened by greater understanding by the experience of the transcendent, we walk with Jesus and one another as we share the Joy of the Eucharist. ♛

# CHAPTER 30

*Fr. Paul Volk and Panama:*

BULLETIN — April 10, 2016

BULLETIN — June 28, 2020

As many of you know, I served here as rector from 2002 till 2007. Upon concluding that time of service, I had a 6 month sabbatical. During the sabbatical, I wrote a book, *Soul Seeking with Paul Volk*.

Fr. Paul Volk was a priest in Kentucky 100 years ago. He was once the pastor of Sts. Peter and Paul Church in Danville. He departed from there in 1895; I began to serve as pastor at Danville in 1995. Fr. Volk was a native of Germany but came to the USA as a missionary to German-speaking Catholics in Kentucky. Most of his ministry in Kentucky was in the area of Owensboro. However, he also organized communities and built churches for the immigrant coal-miners in Eastern Kentucky. In Jellico, he built the first church in Kentucky's Appalachia. The church that he built in East Bernstadt, near London, Ky. is still standing and serves as a historic shrine and location for occasional Masses.

Fr. Volk had the zeal of a missionary and the heart of an adventurer. He became a missionary in Ecuador and eventually ministered for over 20 years in Panama. In Panama he founded and built churches, was a traveling missionary in rural and forest areas, and served as a hospital chaplain for workers as the Panama Canal was being built. He cared particularly for the poor, for those who were victims of racial prejudice, and for those who were downtrodden in any way.

During my sabbatical I traveled throughout Kentucky and Panama to the places where Fr. Volk ministered. I was seeking to understand and be inspired by his life and ministry, and the vestiges of his presence in these areas. And so I wrote the book, which gradually tells the story of Fr. Paul Volk, but also offers some personal reflections and "soul seeking". At the end of each chapter there are a couple of suggested reflection questions because the issues and themes throughout the book are issues and themes common to most Catholics who are "soul-seeking".

The book was self-published and has been twice re-printed. I have a few copies left, and so next weekend I will have a book-signing in Hehman Hall following each Mass. In bookstores, the book has sold for $15.

The proceeds of the book signing will go to our St. Vincent De Paul ministry, to support the rehabilitation of St. Sylvester Church in East Bernstadt, and to supplement the cost of our Year of Mercy banners. ♛

PAUL PRABELL

As this week comes to a close, Friday, July 3, will be the 100th anniversary of the death of Dr. William Gorgas. Dr. Gorgas is famous as the doctor whose leadership made it possible for the Panama Canal to be built.

As an Army physician, he was serving at Ft. Brown, in Southwest Texas in the late 19th century. During his time there a yellow fever epidemic was raging in the area. It was a disease which moved quickly and killed almost half the people who were infected. One of the people he treated was Marie Doughty, the sister-in-law of the camp commander. She was so sick that a burial site had already been chosen for her. Dr. Gorgas, a dedicated Christian, was prepared to offer prayers at her graveside. He himself however, contracted yellow fever and nearly died. So Marie and William were simultaneously sick, convalesced together, and, both not only recovered, but fell in love and married. And Dr. Gorgas was immune then to yellow fever, and he adopted a special mission in life to combat yellow fever.

Dr. Gorgas next served in Cuba as the century was turning. During the Spanish-American War many more soldiers died of yellow fever than from combat. Up till then, yellow fever was regarded as a disease borne by "bad air". In Cuba, Dr. Gorgas drew from the research of Dr. Carlos Finlay, a Cuban doctor, and Walter Reed, who determined that yellow fever and malaria are passed on by mosquitoes. It was quite a battle for Dr. Gorgas to convince other medical professionals that the mosquito was the source of the plague. There are over 2500 different species of mosquitoes, all belonging to three general classifications. One classification carries yellow fever, another carries malaria. (Our Kentucky mosquitoes belong to the third classification and do not bear these diseases.) Dr. Gorgas implemented a sanitation program of screening, fumigation and outlawing open cisterns and standing water. This approach resulted in almost totally wiping out the threats of yellow fever and malaria in Havana.

Dr. Gorgas' next assignment was in Panama, in the area around the city of Colon, at the northern part of the projected canal. To a great extent, it was a city built on a swamp. Yellow fever haunted that part of Panama. Many people departed Panama out of fear; 75 percent of the North Americans who lived there left for safer environments. The French who planned to build the canal left because their workforce was decimated by malaria and particularly by yellow fever. When the U. S. began its work on the canal, Dr. Gorgas was assigned to be the chief medical officer. He applied for a million dollars to protect the workers. He was given $50,000 to do his work. He appealed further, and finally President Theodore Roosevelt and John Stevens, the chief project engineer, made sure that Dr. Gorgas would receive the money he needed for the extensive safety protocol. A veritable sanitation army emerged, draining the swamp, covering the cisterns, treating undrainable waters to prevent larvae from developing, and fumigating every house and other building. Yellow fever was completely eradicated from Panama in two years; and other diseases were greatly reduced...and the work on the canal could proceed.

The most vulnerable workers were men from the nearby Caribbean islands whose heritage was African and whose history was enslavement. Their quarters were the most unsanitary locations and their rate of illness was the greatest. At the same time, by the grace of God, Father Paul Volk was ministering in that part of Panama. A native of Germany, a missionary who built many churches in Central and Eastern Kentucky (including the first churches in Kentucky's Appalachia) he eventually served in Panama

*(Continued on page 120*

*(Continued from page 119)*

for many years. He was stationed in Colon, was appointed by the governor of Panama to serve as chaplain at Colon's hospital for the canal workers, and labored tirelessly among the most neglected and hard core laborers. Meanwhile, he was building a church in Colon, which eventually became its cathedral...and he even worked shifts on the canal construction crews to generate funds for the church. He founded a hospice for sick canal workers and lived in the shanty towns where the laborers lived. He himself had to ward off the sicknesses endemic to the region even as he cared for those who were in the most abject situations.

Dr. Gorgas was honored in life and afterwards, he eventually became Surgeon General of the U.S. Army. Father Volk is revered in Panama and in Western Kentucky, particularly where he founded an Ursuline Sisters' Motherhouse and Boarding School in Owensboro, and he was the founding missionary of several parishes in our own diocese.

There is no record of Father Volk and Doctor Gorgas meeting...but they are linked by the Panama Canal, their dedication to care for vulnerable people in the midst of an epidemic, and their willingness to follow their sense of mission in life. Both Doctor Gorgas and Father Volk exemplify what to do and how to live and give in the midst of an epidemic. ▆

# CHAPTER 31

*Oktoberfest:*

BULLETIN — September 13, 2015

BULLETIN — September 18, 2016

BULLETIN — September 10, 2017

BULLETIN — September 2, 2018

BULLETIN — September 15, 2019

BULLETIN — October 25, 2020

everal years ago a Church theologian, Fr. Teilhard de Chardin, S.J. said that "joy is the most infallible sign of the presence of God." If so, the joy we feel at the time of our Oktoberfest reminds us that God is with us and God is at the center of our lives.

Our Oktoberfest has evolved into an opportunity to celebrate on a grand scale the life that we share and the extensive ministries which we offer. Our Oktoberfest generates much needed resources for our school and our outreach ministries.

The joys of our Oktoberfest can be observed in the light of the Joyful Mysteries of the Rosary.

The first Joyful Mystery of the Rosary is the Annunciation, where Mary is asked to be the mother of God, and she humbly says that she will. The first Oktoberfest Joyful mystery is the cadre of volunteers who have good reasons to say no, but instead say yes as they draw from their faith and love for the parish.

The second Joyful Mystery of the Rosary is the Visitation of Mary and Elizabeth. This is mirrored at the Oktoberfest by the many visitations, conversations, shared stories, mutual encouragement, and pure joy as we welcome visitors and do some joyful catching up with old friends.

The third Joyful Mystery is the birth of Jesus. In the Oktoberfest we see families with babies in strollers and fun events for the small children...but there is also the new life generated as we celebrate new friends and the people who connect or re-connect with our Church.

*Photo by Maureen Guarnieri-Yeager*

The fourth Joyful Mystery of the Rosary refers to the Presentation of Jesus in the temple as Mary and Joseph dedicated their son to God. We might not live out this mystery during the Oktoberfest, but when we see our children's faces and visualize the faces of those served by our outreach ministries, then we find ourselves saying "This is why we work so hard on the Oktoberfest."

The fifth Joyful Mystery is the Finding of Jesus in the temple. Mary and Joseph are concerned that Jesus is lost, but when they find him, he is discussing scripture in the temple with Jewish leaders and scholars Oktoberfest calls for a lot of planning, but always there are some unexpected challenges or some aspect seems to be on the verge of chaos. It is like the sense of order and organization is about to be lost. But always, things have a way of being worked out.

A Jesuit maxim is to find God in every experience of life. As we keep our eyes and hearts open, we will notice God in our joyous Oktoberfest. ♔

In the aftermath of our Oktoberfest we have much to be thankful for and many reasons to be reflective. We are very grateful for our leaders, our many volunteers on Friday and Saturday, the many volunteers who worked through the week in gradually setting up the tents and booths and those who formed the take-down and clean-up crews on Sunday. We are grateful for the generosity of our sponsors and their dedication to Christ the King. It was wonderful to be part of the sea of people who came for the good time which our Oktoberfest offers. Our music groups spoke glowingly of the crowds and their receptiveness. The food, the games, and the children's activities offered a good variety of enjoyable options. We are grateful for all who took chances on the raffle and congratulate our winner, Heather Yaste.

It is difficult to believe that any of our Oktoberfest nights ever had more people than we had on Friday. On Saturday evening, we were humbled by the violent storm...but also very grateful that the storm passed through rather quickly. Our needs pale in comparison to farmers affected by droughts, people rendered homeless by floods, neighborhoods ravaged by wildfire. We truly are vulnerable to our natural elements to which God gives freedom and humanity occasionally alters by our abuse of our resources. If nothing else, our Saturday storm connected us with the lack of control we have of our weather, a powerlessness shared by rich and poor.

On the Thursday before the Oktoberfest, the 5:30 p.m. Mass had a special invitation to Oktoberfest workers to come and pray our way into the festival. Our intercessory prayers at the Mass included...

- for the safety and joy of all who come to the Oktoberfest as partakers and volunteers
- with gratitude for our many workers and leader at our Oktoberfest
- for the rain our community needs...but not during the Oktoberfest
- with gratitude for the ministry of Father Murphy and his continual prayers from heaven
- for those who come here this weekend needing to find a Church to call home...we prayed to the Lord

Now we rest a bit...we savor a fantastic Oktoberfest and wait for the final results.

We trust that it has been a strong financial success, helping our Church, school, and outreach ministries. We trust that our Oktoberfest festival has been a gift to our parish and community. And we trust that our Oktoberfest has been a tribute to the can-do spirit of good people working together as a team to spread the Good News and the joy of who we are at Christ the King. ♛

*Photo by Maureen Guarnieri-Yeager*

This week there will be a flurry of activity as we prepare for our annual Oktoberfest on Friday and Saturday. We look forward to the joy, the crowds, the community spirit, and the opportunity to bring people together from all parts of Lexington, from all walks of life, and from places beyond. We are all thankful for the work being done by our Oktoberfest leaders and the many volunteers who are surfacing. The Oktoberfest gives us a picture of a parish united by our desire to celebrate, to offer hospitality, and ultimately to generate needed resources for our parish, school, and outreach ministries.

Concurrently we are gearing up for our Light of the World parish retreat which is only a few weeks away. A parish retreat is an opportunity for every participant to look at their lives, to deepen their prayer, and to make any changes which need to be made. But a parish retreat also brings together the richness of the diverse members of our parish community. Many people can look back on their involvement in a parish retreat as the beginning of some very important friendships and the first step into a more involved and joyful use of their gifts for the good of the parish and community.

In a vibrant parish like ours, there are some aspects of a parish festival which are part of the dynamics of a parish retreat.

A parish festival and a parish retreat both call for planning and a core group of leaders to generate more involvement and participation and they call for a quality presentation.

The Oktoberfest continues to evolve...we have some wonderful music

*Photo by Maureen Guarnieri-Yeager*

performers, the games and children's activities are well-organized, we have added the Oktoberdash to the venue, we will have delicious food and beverages, our booths, raffles and other stations are ready to offer a variety of ways to have fun. Research, planning, and community involvement are keys to our success.

Ministry to a parish's spiritual life and our shared journey with Jesus draws from those same elements of research, planning and the work of a team. As we offer the Light of the World Retreat we believe that this retreat has the kind of approach that will lead the participants to feel the joy of living the Gospel, that it will set our hearts afire, and that it will lead many parishioners to encounter Jesus and fellow members of the parish on an entirely different level than ever before.

There are other common points between a parish festival and a parish retreat. In each case, we realize that our efforts are reliant on God's blessings...as we plead for good weather, as we open ourselves to gifts we did not realize we had, as we see and hear the unexpected giftedness of those around us. Both a festival and a retreat involve work and joy...both lead us to reach out to our God when we are at our limits, and both are fundamentally about an encounter...an encounter with God, an encounter with the people of our community, and an encounter with a Holy Spirit-implanted gifts which have been kept below the surface. ♛

Christ the King has been part of the Diocese of Lexington, since its inception 30 years ago. But prior to that, our parish was part of the Diocese of Covington, dating from the parish's founding in 1945. The Diocese of Covington is just across the Ohio River from Cincinnati. Cincinnati is an old city with German roots and character. Cincinnati is the location of the second largest Oktoberfest celebration in the world, a bit behind Munich's mammoth event. Cincinnati, (and Northern Kentucky), are characterized by the high percentage of German Catholic citizens and many Catholic Churches.

For some time, the Catholic culture within territory of Eastern and Central Kentucky was significantly influenced by the Greater Cincinnati/German Catholic spirit. Many of the priests who served at Christ the King have been natives of Northern Kentucky and of German descent. It is no wonder that here at our Cathedral, our primary parish festival is the Oktoberfest.

Many people associate Oktoberfests with beer. The original German Oktoberfests were festivals of gratitude and thanksgiving for the fruitful harvests which would provide food for the up-coming winter. But it was also an occasion to sample the bock beer which had been brewed from the local grains. The bock beer was particularly regarded as being high in nutrients and would provide a kind of "back-up" if food ran short. In fact, monks in Bavaria drank their home brew as a kind of smoothie or "Ensure" during times of fasting.

History tells us that Martin Luther appreciated a good beer. For several weeks, members of our congregation and Faith Lutheran Church have been participating in a dialogue about inter-faith issues. This Wednesday, there will be a pot-luck supper as we celebrate the fellowship that has developed. Please do not guess what I will be bringing to the pot-luck supper.

We live in an era which is commemorating the 50th anniversary of the Second Vatican Council. German bishops and theologians were very influential in the discussions and writing of the documents of the Council. Among the most revered of the German theologians was Karl Rahner, a priest of the Jesuit order. Karl Rahner was a prolific writer and teacher, a scholar well-versed in a broad range of areas, and valued the collaborative approach that was at the heart of the council's proceedings. Among the insights which he brought to the council are that he taught that God's grace does not exclude anyone, he advocated for the re-introduction of the permanent diaconate, he maintained that the Church has a basic sacramental nature, he spoke strongly of the collegial relationship of the pope and the bishops when they are gathered together, and he emphasized Mary's relation to the Church. He had much influence on many of the documents of the Second Vatican Council, including those on the Church, ministry, and the Bible.

Additionally, Karl Rahner loved carnivals.

And so as we prepare for next weekend's Oktoberfest, we seek to serve our parish and community with a fun time which generates funds for our parish, our school and our outreach ministries, we give thanks for the fruitfulness of this past year, we build on the sense of unity of our team of volunteers and, we welcome guests from many different places. But also, we give thanks for the German spirit at the soul of all Oktoberfests, and we give thanks for the spirit and prayers of great Irish priests like Msgr. O'Neill and Father Murphy. ⛪

This upcoming weekend marks the 10th Oktoberfest at which I have been present as the rector. I remember my first Oktoberfest. The standard procedure was that priests always sang a few songs on stage. So I organized a group of priests, brought in a few ringers, wore a few little bit of Elvis apparel and wigs, and sang a few Elvis Presley hits and a few songs of the 60s. The good news is that the crowd was pleased; the bad news is that it wasn't much of a crowd. Those Oktoberfest priestly performances are referred to as the days of the singing cowboys. As you know, the quality of the musical entertainment has increased by leaps and bounds.

In a way, Oktoberfest history parallels the technological progress of communication. In 2002, when the winning ticket of the car raffle was pulled, the cry went out, "Does anyone have a cell phone, so that we can call the winner?" One person had a cell phone that night 17 years ago.

I served as rector here from 2002-2007, then served for seven and a half years at Morehead's Jesus Our Savior parish and its missions. But before going to Morehead, I had a six month sabbatical; three months of which I spent at a priests' renewal program in San Francisco, with about 25 other priests from throughout the English-speaking world. At the mid-juncture of our program, in October, we had a party. I was pleased that the group followed my suggestion, and had an Oktoberfest party. Even though it was on an adapted level, the key Oktoberfest spirit(s) defined our California celebration.

*Photo by Maureen Guarnieri-Yeager*

Over the years, I continue to be grateful for the volume of volunteers who emerge from the ranks of our parishioners. I am particularly grateful when involvement in the Oktoberfest serves as a stimulus to be involved in the life of the parish in many other ways. Every year a new team of leaders joins the veterans and they give of many hours to organizing, doing the last week preparations, and keeping things running smoothly on Friday and Saturday. I am amazed at the new developments worked out every year. And I am always deeply appreciative of the calmness and skill as our team responds to the inevitable unexpected challenges.

Oktoberfest is a time of prayer. We pray for good weather. We ask our beloved Fr. Bob Murphy to offer his powerful prayers for good weather. We realize God has more important things to do, but we trust that God will bless us and give us the weather we need for a successful Oktoberfest. The Oktoberfest weather concern leads us to a spirit of solidarity with people throughout the world whose livelihoods and very lives depend on the right kind of weather.

We are in the midst of a significant Capital Campaign. We are preparing for our next big run with this campaign. The Capital Campaign is focused on repairing, rehabing and renewing the infrastructure of the buildings of our campus. So too, the Oktoberfest is concerned with our community infrastructure; building up not only the capital we have for our ministries, but fortifying the spirit and joy of giving ourselves to living and spreading the Good News. Just as the Capital Campaign is a united effort for our Church and school, so too does the Oktoberfest bring together the spirit and joy of people intensely invested in our parish and school, in effect reminding us of our unified ministries.

So this Friday, as I offer my 10th Oktoberfest Beer Barrel Blessing, I will pray with you that this year's Oktoberfest will be a success in every way that we need it to be. ♟

C incinnati's Oktoberfest is the largest Oktoberfest celebration in North America and is second only to that held in Munich. This year it was dubbed "In ze haus"; it was virtual. Restaurants and taverns had limited capacity; take out boxes of German food was the typical fare; toasts of "ein prosit" were on-line; and the world's largest chicken dance was one more zoom event. I have not yet received a report on how the annual race of the wiener dogs was conducted (usually, it is 100 dachshunds, each wrapped in some kind of hot dog bun paraphernalia.)

And so we here at Christ the King are not alone as we celebrate this up-coming Friday our virtual Oktoberfest. Thanks to all who have been working faithfully and creatively to make this year's Oktoberfest an event to remember and an event that will offer significant financial support for our parish and school. I encourage you to honor our Oktoberfest with your own choice of German food and beverage and to offer a toast with us at 7 p.m. on Friday evening.

Whatever we do this year is groundwork for Oktoberfest 2021; and yet we also have plenty of reasons and plenty of ways to celebrate. As the up-coming week transpires, it is scheduled to be a week of spires...as our refurbished bell, tower, steeple and cross are re-planted on our church. We are grateful for our team of staff, volunteers and contractors who have approached this effort with great wisdom, resolve, respect and reverence.

Oktoberfest is an event where we annually host one of our largest gatherings of people here on our grounds. Our most largely attended Masses of the year are on Christmas Eve. We are beginning now to make plans for Christmas Masses which will be safe by means of social distancing and yet welcoming for everyone who seeks to come. It seems reasonable to treat them as ticketed Masses. We will be considering secondary locations on campus for Masses. And, for sure, we will need a spike in our number of ushers. These ushers will need at least a short training session. We do not expect that Christmas ushers will serve as ushers for the long haul. This is really a ministry...keeping everyone who comes safe! It is a ministry which will call for some sacrifice in this very unusual and dangerous year. The sacrifice includes not being able to sit with your family at Christmas Mass. Some folks who will be ushers will come to one Christmas Mass with their family and then serve as an usher at another Mass. Ushering at Christmas this year could be one of the most special gifts you can give the Lord to celebrate his coming into our world.

At this particular time, right now, we are in need of more ushers, especially for our 5 p.m. Sunday Mass. We are grateful for our ushers who have been serving at our Masses, but some have moved or have had other commitments emerge; and some are on the verge of burning out. The intensity of the ushering ministry will not last forever; nor will the pandemic last forever. But the way the disease can spread, and the way our Church is laid out, and the way our assembly varies from week to week call for this very important and health-protective ministry of ushering.

I ask you who are reading this message to prayerfully consider becoming part of our ushers team at least for Christmas and possibly on a "regular" basis. If you can help, please contact Mike and Irene Nuzzo at (412) 848-9141 or minuzzo@roadrunner.com ♕

# CHAPTER 32

*History of Our Diocese:*

BULLETIN — March 4, 2018

BULLETIN — March 1, 2020

Human development theories refer to a person's 30s as the time of becoming our own person, of solidifying our identity. Perhaps it is the same for our Diocesan Church, and therefore, our Cathedral parish.

This past Friday, March 2 was the 30th anniversary of the dedication of our cathedral, the beginning of our diocese of Lexington, and the installation of our first bishop, J. Kendrick Williams. Our magnificent church, built with the mindset that it would someday be a cathedral, fulfilled its destiny. Just as with the Sacraments of Baptism, Confirmation, and Ordination, the Chrism Oil was used on March 2, 1988, embedded in our walls as our sacred environment moved to its next stage as a conduit of the gifts of the Holy Spirit.

The Diocese of Lexington was formed from the central, southern and eastern counties of the diocese of Covington and seven western counties of the Louisville Archdiocese. Bishop Williams was a native of Central Kentucky, served there and in the city of Louisville and then was Auxiliary Bishop of Covington, so he knew the land, the culture, and many people in this new diocese. The rationale for the new diocese was related to the difficulty of adequately ministering to the three diverse demographic groups which formed the Diocese of Covington...strongly Catholic Northern Kentucky, the mission territory of Eastern Kentucky, and the burgeoning area of Central Kentucky. The Lexington Diocese began with the understanding that we are a mission diocese and that the connection between Lexington and Eastern Kentucky would be a much stronger connection than that of Covington and Eastern Kentucky.

Priests like Father Ray and me had our roots in Northern Kentucky and had been serving as priests of the Diocese of Covington. The standard procedure was that if we were serving in 1988 within the territory of the new diocese, then we were going to be priests of the Lexington Diocese. All of my assignments had been in the territory of the new diocese, so my heart was here. I enjoyed the mix of Christianity and the freer spirit generated by the high percentage of Catholics who had moved to Kentucky from other parts of the country. In my experience, Catholicism, and life in general in the Bluegrass and Appalachia have a different "feel" than in Northern Kentucky.

Over these 30 years, the influx of Hispanic migrants has changed the texture of the Church in our diocese. Latino Catholics and Catholics from many other countries are touching us by their faith and reminding us of our call to be a world Church. Certainly a new demographic has arisen. Concurrently, we have seen a sharp rise in Catholics who "do not practice their faith."

I recall that an initial concern was that the Lexington Diocese might not have enough priests and priestly vocations to serve the Church as needed. We have been helped by priests from religious orders and priests from other countries...but we do need more priests coming from within our own territory. A second concern was whether we would have the financial resources to support our Church, its many ministries, and our parishes and missions. That is a challenge, but it seems to be a challenge felt throughout the nation. A third concern was whether our Diocesan church would have a sense of unity in our missionary focus; whether we in the Bluegrass would have a heart for the Church and people of Appalachia. Strikingly as the years have gone on, missionary work to fellow Catholics has emerged as a primary aspect of the Church's ministry in every diocese in our nation.

The questions of a diocese's identity or even a cathedral's identity are important questions in an era when there is much concern about Catholics embracing our identity as Catholics. Identity is chosen, it is a reaction, and it is the embrace of a gift. You and I will be part of the answer. ▟

This Monday, March 2 is the anniversary of the establishment of the Diocese of Lexington in 1988. On the same day the diocese was established, Christ the King became the cathedral of the diocese. Our church was packed with guests and parishioners as many bishops, priests, deacons and religious and dignitaries from our region and beyond were in attendance. Bishop Kendrick Williams was consecrated as the founding bishop of our diocese and there were special prayers as our church itself was blessed. So this Monday we celebrate the anniversary of the diocese and our cathedral.

It was the realization of the dream of Msgr. O'Neill that Christ the King would someday be a cathedral.

Prior to 1988 the city of Lexington and much of Central and Eastern Kentucky were part of the Diocese of Covington. Located on the Ohio River Covington was the largest city in the three county area of Kenton, Boone and Campbell Counties. This area had and still has a fairly high percentage of its citizens who are Catholic. It has a high concentration of parishes and Church activity. Prior to 1988, Church leaders described the diversity of the three regions in the Diocese of Covington, and therefore three different demographics and sets of needs. The three regions are Northern Kentucky, Central Kentucky and Eastern Kentucky. Church leaders felt like they could not give sufficient attention to ministry in Central and Eastern Kentucky because of their focus on (and their immersion in) the area where the most Catholics resided.

Concurrently, many parish leaders in our Bluegrass and mission territories felt a bit neglected and yearned for the autonomy that their own diocese could provide. One important aspect of the rationale for the change was that Lexington and the Bluegrass Catholics would connect with and offer support and kinship with the missionary ministry in Eastern Kentucky. It was ultimately a decision of the pope to establish this new diocese; Bishop Hughes of Covington and Archbishop Kelly of Louisville presented the case for a new diocese. Many who were involved in the life of the Church in Kentucky had speculated on this development for many years; so it was not a great surprise. Later in 1988, Knoxville was established as a diocese taking the Eastern portion of the Diocese of Nashville, for precisely the same reasons as Lexington was established.

We continue to grow as a diocese where we Catholics are a distinct minority, even here in the city of Lexington. Our Diocesan Appeal calls for us to embrace and support the missionary ministry of the church in Eastern Kentucky, where many of our counties, Catholics comprise less than one percent of the population. The challenges and blessings of our life as the Diocese of Lexington have evolved in ways that no one could predict; and yet we trust that God's Holy Spirit is guiding us as we move forward.

I encourage you to attend Mass and offer special prayers on Monday for our Diocesan Church. I will be at the Federal prison, offering Masses that day, but our diocesan ministry will be in our prayers.

This year as we celebrate the 75th anniversary of our parish's founding, it is good to note the parallels between the establishment of a diocese and the establishment of a parish. Grassroots people speak of a need; they and Church leaders envision the future (as much of Chevy Chase was farmland in 1945); a Church authority makes a decision; membership changes (our pioneers to a great extent had been members of St. Peter's parish); and a new, exciting and unpredictable life begins....The Spirit of God strikes again! ♛

# CHAPTER 33

*75 Years as a Parish:*

BULLETIN — November 8, 2015

BULLETIN — January 5, 2020

BULLETIN — March 29, 2020

In two weeks, on November 22, on the feast of Christ the King, we will be celebrating the 70th anniversary of the establishment of our parish. In 1925 the *Feast of Christ the King* was established by Pope Pius XI partly as a reminder to a world threatened by dictators and totalitarian governments that there is one primary king of all time and all places — Jesus Christ. Our parish was founded just as World War II was concluding. Our first church building was a pre-fabricated building which was a war surplus item.

Our first pastor was Fr. George O'Bryan. Due to health problems he had to resign after less than a year at the helm. Then Fr. Richard Garland O'Neill, a Lexington native, became pastor. At the time he became pastor, Fr. O'Neill was serving as chaplain at the Oaks, a rehabilitation facility that was located on the grounds of the present St. Joseph's Hospital parking lot. This chaplaincy was regarded as a "light" assignment for Fr. O'Neill, who needed some time to rebuild his strength following his tenure as a high school teacher in Northern Kentucky.

Fr. O'Neill quickly grew into his new assignment and served as pastor here until 1968. During this time our church, school and rectory (the present O'Neill Center) were built. Fr. O'Neill was elevated to the status of monsignor. As early as 1947 the parish bulletin had a rendering of how the Church would look when it would be built, and the result was true to this presentation. Edward Schulte, a Cincinnati-based architect worked closely with Msgr. O'Neill as the plans developed, the parish grew, and the necessary funds were generated and finally, the Church was built in 1967.

Until 1988, Lexington was part of the Diocese of Covington, and its chancery office and cathedral were in Covington, across from Cincinnati, fairly far removed from the Bluegrass and Appalachian regions. Msgr. O'Neill had a vision the Christ the King would eventually become a cathedral. However, there is no record whether he felt that we would be a "southern" co-cathedral for Covington, or that he felt the offices for Covington would be moved to a more central location, or that he felt a new diocese was inevitable.

Edward Schulte was an architect who built several Catholic churches, primarily in Cincinnati and Northern Kentucky. In his autobiography, *The Lord Was My Client*, he describes our church as the crown jewel of his career.

In 1957, another Schulte-designed church, Our Lord Christ the King, was dedicated in suburban Cincinnati. This church has many of the same features as our church. Our pastoral team plans to make a day trip this Friday to see Our Lord Christ the King Church.

Meanwhile, plans are continuing to develop for our celebration of our 70th anniversary in two weeks. We will have a historic display, Mass at 11:15 a.m. with Bishop Stowe, and a parish pot-luck luncheon afterwards. I hope you will be able to join us as we celebrate our feast, honor our memories, and sow seeds for the future. ♛

As the year 2020 begins, we inaugurate a commemoration of the 75th year of our parish's life. Christ the King was established in the spring of 1945. Father George O'Bryan was the first pastor. In July the parish boundaries were established (Parish boundaries were more important in those days, but less than 100 Catholic households lived in our area.) The first Mass of the Catholic community of Christ the King parish was held on July 22 at St. Catherine's Academy, on North Limestone, with less than 60 households represented. Upon Fr. O'Bryan's incapacity due to illness, Father Richard Garland O'Neill became pastor in August. Our land was purchased in November of 1945 for $29,000....Fr. O'Neill insisted to officials of the Diocese of Covington that the parish would grow so much that we would need the entire block.

I look forward to the ways we can celebrate our 75 years of history throughout 2020. I encourage you to offer ideas and also corrections or refinements to the historical picture which is being offered. Below are the first two paragraphs of an article in the *Lexington Herald-Leader's* Bluegrass section. It was written around 1988 by Anne Cassidy, who grew up in Christ the King's parish and school. The article is entitled, "The Little Church That Could."

"Forty-two years ago, on a few acres of Bluegrass meadow, a pre-fabricated frame church proclaimed the beginnings of a new Catholic parish in Lexington. Now the Pope has named that same parish the head of a new diocese, and Christ the King church is now Christ the King Cathedral.

New churches come and go; cathedrals are something else entirely. But in a funny sort of way, no one seems surprised that 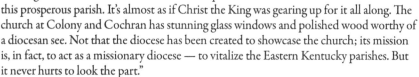 the long arm of Rome would reach out and tap this prosperous parish. It's almost as if Christ the King was gearing up for it all along. The church at Colony and Cochran has stunning glass windows and polished wood worthy of a diocesan see. Not that the diocese has been created to showcase the church; its mission is, in fact, to act as a missionary diocese — to vitalize the Eastern Kentucky parishes. But it never hurts to look the part."

Before there was the magnificent church, there was the pre-fab building and its second and third parts. But even before the pre-fab building, there was the community of parishioners...the parish family.

The Christmas season is a time of humble beginnings centered around the manger in Bethlehem. It is an apt time to recall the humble beginnings of our small, but tight-knit community whose first dwelling was a pre-fabricated building, St. Sear and Roebuck, as Father O'Neill called it. On that first Epiphany feast, wise men from the East recognized the greatness of the little boy whom they were seeking. 1900 years later, many skilled people came to Lexington from the East, especially with IBM ("I've been moved") and they recognized the great potential of their new home area and their little parish.

"Do you see what I see..." This is the beginning line of a popular Christmas song. Periodically, through 2020, we will all be invited to see the history of our parish, to see the presence of the Holy Spirit throughout the years, and to see the presence of God's grace as we make our journey together, seeking to follow and live in the radiance of the light of Christ. ♛

The year 2020 will be etched in our memories as the year of the Coronavirus outbreak. But it is also the year of the 75th anniversary of the founding of our parish. And also the 75th anniversary of the conclusion of World War II. The USA was a key military force in that war. World history would probably read much differently if we had not gotten involved. Thankfully, our mainland USA was not a locale for battles between armed forces; we did not face the destruction which Europe, Asia, North Africa, Japan and the Pacific Islands experienced. And yet the face of America changed because of World War II.

Many of our men and women served in the military; on an unprecedented level, women entered the workforce. Nationally, more than 10,000 manufacturing companies altered their production. For example, in Cincinnati, Baldwin Piano Company made wooden wings for mail planes; Crosley Radio made transmitters for military communications; the dressmaking company, Fashion Frocks made parachutes; U.S. Playing Cards decorated the backgrounds of their cards with the silhouettes of enemy aircraft; and Procter and Gamble loaded and packaged millions of ammunition shells monthly.

Our nation rationed meat, coffee, sugar, gasoline and shoes. A maximum speed limit of 35 miles an hour was imposed, people were called upon to car-pool. A coupon system was developed regarding how much could be spent of certain commodities. Recycling scrap metal was a very important strategy.

Patriotism was high. Our churches prayed for soldiers from their congregations and prayed for victory and for peace. There were many governmental and Church initiated responses to the poor and to those whose security was threatened by the stress of the war. During this time Catholic Relief Services emerged to care for those displaced by the war, but also in the war's aftermath, to help in the rebuilding of many lives and cities which had been bombed and otherwise damaged or even destroyed during the war. Following the war, the United Nations emerged, as an organization dedicated to peace and conflict resolution, and within the Catholic Church, Pax Christi began its ministry of advocating world-wide non-violence. Following the war, amicable relations among the warring nations progressed, even as the Cold War was dawning.

For our nation, the time following the close of World War II was a time of optimism and growth. It was the time of industrial growth, the time of the G.I. Bill, a time of emerging suburbs, and a time when Christ the King parish was born in the country-side of Southeastern Lexington.

I offer these reflections in the light of our anniversary...and in the light of our national war on the pandemic Coronavirus...this is a time when we need to be dedicated and unified.

We need to be vigilant...we need to be wary of a premature declaration of victory... we need to be patient...we need to find ways to be at peace as we live in a new normal manner...We do need all of us working together...we do need to work together...we do need to make sure we have enough, but also that there is enough for everyone...we need to trust the joy of caring for and helping one another...we do need to make some adaptations and sacrifices...but we can do it...together...throughout Lexington...throughout Kentucky...throughout our nation...throughout the world. 📖

# CHAPTER 34

*Our Beautiful Cathedral:*

BULLETIN — March 24, 2019

The world will be saved by beauty", maintains Prince Myshkin, who was stricken with epilepsy but is the brave and wise hero of the Fyodor Dostoevsky classic, *The Idiot*. The recent memoir of Dorothy Day by her grand-daughter, Kate Hennessey is entitled, *The World Will Be Saved by Beauty*. The encyclical entitled *The Light of Faith*, begun by Pope Benedict and finished by Pope Francis refer to the impact on the faith of Prince Myshkin when he contemplated a graphic artistic portrayal of Jesus dead in the tomb.

Aleksandr Solzhenitsyn, a famous Soviet dissident and Nobel laureate, used the same quote in a Nobel speech as he referred to the transcendental qualities of truth, goodness and beauty, all different and yet all interconnected. He suggested that evil can eclipse truth and goodness, but evil cannot destroy beauty. And therefore, art in its many manifestations can lead us back to truth and goodness.

Throughout the ages, art has led us to encounter Jesus, Mary and the saints and their message to us regarding how to live with integrity and joy. Christian philosophers have referred to Jesus as the ultimate expression of goodness, truth and beauty. Even artistic expressions of the passion and death of Jesus reveal the extent of God's love for us, as Prince Myshkin has attested.

"The world will be saved by beauty"...beauty leads us to rediscover truth and goodness, beauty reveals the face of God and the heart of Jesus, there is the beauty and attractiveness of people living in harmony with God...That is the theme of the song by Ann Wilson "How beautiful is the Body of Christ"...Isaiah 52:7 declares "How beautiful upon the mountains are the feet of those who bring glad tidings, announcing peace, bearing good news, announcing salvation and saying to Zion, 'Your God is King'".

Over the years I have served here, countless people have commented on the beauty of our cathedral. Many hearts have been moved by our stained glass windows, our sanctuary and primary cross, the stations, the Adoration chapel, Our Lady of Guadalupe's chapel, the statues, and even the massive but noble "feel" of our church. Recently, one of our parishioners told me how he comes to make a visit daily to receive inspiration and direction for his day. You and I know that this man's feelings are shared by many others.

That is why we are having our Capital Campaign. The beauty of our cathedral is dependent on the internal structures...the leak-less roofs and windows, the re-done mortar, the efficiency of HVAC systems, the tower which is a safe and strong symbol of God's soaring majesty. That is why we enter this next chapter of our Capital Campaign, our *Run for the Roses*, a drive within our campaign, a run that will culminate with the Derby and the Derby eve party we will have on May 3. Our goal is to stabilize our cathedral, to enhance its beauty, and to trust that beauty to touch our souls and the souls of generations to come. I encourage you to recall how the beauty of our cathedral has touched your life and how it has led you to seek truth, to value goodness, to connect with Christian friends, and to encounter Jesus.

# CHAPTER 35

*The Rosary:*

BULLETIN — May 1, 2016

BULLETIN — May 3, 2020

One of the contributions of St. John Paul II has been the establishment of the *Luminous Mysteries* as a fourth set of meditations while praying the rosary. The mysteries of the rosary invite us to meditate not only on the life of Jesus, but also on our own lives.

The sorrowful mysteries focus on the passion and death of Jesus. For people who are feeling sorrow because of illness, family problems, financial difficulties, loneliness, crime, grief, impending death or some kind of injustice...the sorrowful mysteries give a voice to their pain, and they reassure us that we are not alone, that Jesus experienced sorrow and pain, and that Mary will help us by her motherly care and her fruitful prayer.

The glorious mysteries focus on eternal life, highlighting the Resurrection of Jesus and the Assumption of Mary into heaven. The glorious mysteries remind us of the blessings of everlasting life with the Lord. But in the human situations of grief, pain and anger...the glory can be emphasized too intensely and too quickly. We need time to experience our feelings and to trust that the whirlwind of desolation and consolation will eventually stabilize.

> *Our baptisms have made us part of a community, a family of wounded healers on a pilgrimage with the Lord.*

Here is where the luminous mysteries of the rosary offer a bridge. In the midst of the sorrows of our lives, it is helpful to reflect on the light which the presence of God has brought, to recall the power of special blessings, and to allow our darkness to be illuminated by the occasions of grace which are part of ordinary Christian lives.

The first of the luminous mysteries is the Baptism of Jesus. Our baptisms have made us part of a community, a family of wounded healers on a pilgrimage with the Lord. Most of us have seen miracles, whether they have been water turned into wine (second luminous mystery) or some other unexplainable blessing, such as cold relationships reconciled, unexpected healings, or deliverance from an addiction. In the third luminous mystery, like the early apostles, we are invited to a special relationship with Jesus, even if we feel we have not deserved it. We have all had or witnessed transfiguration moments (fourth luminous mystery), mountaintop experiences when we or another have radiated our full potential.

The fifth luminous mystery is the institution of the Eucharist. Jesus sets in motion the blessing of the Mass...where time after time we receive Christ into our lives. This weekend as we celebrate the First Communion of our children, we recall the impact of receiving Holy Communion throughout our lives, and how Jesus in the Eucharist helps us to make the transition from sorrow to peace, from darkness to glory, from desolation to consolation. ♕

As we enter the month of May, we begin the month with Mass at 8 a.m. on Friday, May 1. On May 1 in 1945 our parish was instituted by a decree from the Bishop of the Diocese of Covington. So we will have a special spirit of commemoration in Friday's Mass. Following the Mass, there will be a May Crowning presentation by children from our school. These occasions of "virtual prayer" will lead us into the month of May...a month when we all hope to begin to take our first steps as we seek to re-open our world. I encourage you to draw strength from the intercession and example of the Blessed Virgin as we go through our next month of uncertainty.

Mary is the mother of Jesus; she is the mother of the Church; she is our mother. Mary is the ideal of all mothers. A good mother wants her sons and daughters to be free, to live life with no unnecessary restrictions...but a good mother also wants her sons and daughters to be safe, to be patient, to be prudent, and to persevere with the important yet difficult decisions which keep them and others safe. A good mother realizes that life can be hard but that compassion, care and a sense of trust will lead her sons and daughters to work together as part of a community response. A good mother teaches her sons and daughters that their care and generosity need to extend beyond their biological family and extend to the entire human family in their particular cases of struggle.

Part of our light as we journey through the darkness of the pandemic is PRAYER. I encourage you to pray the rosary every day during May. If you are at home as a family, I encourage you to pray it together. Mary knows what we are going through; in fact, she has had similar experiences.

*Photo by Maureen Guarnieri-Yeager*

The joyful mysteries begin on a less than joyful note as Mary is overwhelmed with the UNEXPECTED — she has conceived by the Holy Spirit and she will become the Mother of God. She and Elizabeth support one another in their times of unexpected pregnancies. There is the ultimate highlight of Divine Love for humanity as Jesus is born. But there is also the portent of suffering as the prophet predicts suffering at the time of the child Jesus' presentation, and then there is the challenge to let go, as the teen Jesus gets "lost" in Jerusalem, being about his Heavenly Father's business.

As we pray the *Luminous Mysteries* of the Rosary, we cannot help but envision Mary's joy, pride and wonder as Jesus goes about his ministry. Even today, Mary rejoices with the best work that we do as members of our parish, as we go about our work, and as we live as good neighbors and members of our community. Mary will help us all as we eventually "turn the lights back on" and re-open, and as we offer assistance to those for whom the return to normal does not seem possible.

*(Continued on page 142)*

*(Continued from page 141)*

The Sorrowful Mysteries of the Rosary presage our pandemic suffering. For so many victims and their families it is the way of the Cross...there is the agony in the hospitals and funeral homes. Mary holds us and shares in our confusion and rage at the unfairness of the ordeal we face. As the Stations of the Cross suggest, Mary meets and consoles us in our suffering as we carry our crosses. Mary grieves deeply as she holds the bodies of her deceased children. And yet those words of Jesus from the cross still resonate as the Mother of Jesus is called by Jesus to care for the beloved disciple...and also for the untold number of beloved disciples who continue to need her assistance.

The Glorious Mysteries lead us to see Mary standing with families as they welcome loved ones home from the hospital, encouraging and inspiring all who are working on vaccines and cures, and also helping us all to make good decisions regarding our safety and that of others. The Glorious Mysteries suggest the picture of Mary sharing in the triumph of Jesus rising from the dead and sharing in the triumph of the eventual post-pandemic era. Mary will encourage each and every one of us to trust and to draw from the gifts of the Holy Spirit and she reminds us by her Assumption and Coronation that the goal of life on earth is to eventually be with The Trinity, and with her, and with the angels and saints in eternal glory.

Mary helps us to trust God and God's grace as we day by day make our way through the desert of the pandemic to the place of freedom, health, and the renewal which the lessons of this spring are teaching us. ♛

# CHAPTER 36

*St. Francis:*

BULLETIN — October 4, 2020

A nnually we celebrate the Feast of St. Francis with a pet blessing. St. Francis loved all of nature. He is an inspiration for us as we give and receive affection from our pets, and as we care for them, as their personalities delight us. Pets remind us of the cycle of life and death and they draw joy, playfulness and tenderness from so many of us. Pets have a way of soothing the troubled soul.

Certainly during the pandemic, pets have been much appreciated companions. As I walk through our neighborhood I see folks of all ages taking their dog for a walk. I will be very surprised if any of our neighborhood dogs are overweight.

Francis of fact and legend is famous for taming the wolf of Gubbio and leading the people of that village to adopt the wolf as a pet. Francis preached to birds. When he created creches to honor the coming of the Christ-child into the world, it was important for Francis to make sure that sheep, cows, oxen and sheep dogs were present as part of the welcoming entourage.

Devotees of St. Francis commemorate October 3-4 as the time of the *Transitus* of St. Francis, the time of his death, the time of the culmination of his life, the time of his birth into eternal life. His biographers tell us that Francis was blind and in much pain at the end of his life. And yet he had a spirit of joy as his life on earth was coming to an end. He asked that two of his brothers sing to him The Canticle of the Sun, as it included praise for "Sister Death", an inevitable part of life. He prayed the psalms and encouraged those by his side to join him in prayer. He asked that the Passion and Resurrection of Jesus be read to him from the Gospel of John. He asked that one of his friends bring him some almond cookies to share with all those attending him. St. Francis entered eternal life on Saturday, October 3, 1226.

The heroic and joyful way that Francis embraced his death is counter to our very common fear of death. And yet it is in character with this great saint, this man of faith, this man whose simple faith is full of richness...and complexity. His conversion followed the imprisonment which culminated his short and unsuccessful stint as a soldier. His relationship with his father degenerated into estrangement. He misread God's call to rebuild the Church as a call to do exterior church repairs. He was a courageous idealist who made a pilgrimage to talk with the Muslim sultan about the need for peace during the Crusades. He was blessed with the stigmata. He was never ordained, yet preached and blessed throughout Italy. He attracted many followers and founded three religious orders which took the Church from the monasteries and cathedrals to the streets! He cared for the poor and espoused the importance of poverty. He exemplified love for the world, acceptance of everyone, and belief in the power of God. He was joyful and deep, a searcher who imparted wisdom, and a humble man who is one of our greatest saints. ▲

# CHAPTER 37

*Sometimes Asking for Money!:*

BULLETIN — October 29, 2017

BULLETIN — July 1, 2018

BULLETIN — September 30, 2018

BULLETIN — November 17, 2019

This is the weekend when we kick-off our Capital Campaign to respond to the need that our parish complex has for repairs, replacements and renewal. It is a campaign to generate pledges and donations over a three year period to address our many needs. Since our cathedral was built, we have had drives to provide the funds to further develop our facilities and to thus expand our ministry. But at the same time, we have not focused on the needs of our church, school and office space for major maintenance. During recent months we have been offering tours and videos which tell the story of our needs. Now is the time for us to begin our response as a community.

I believe that our response begins with our appreciation of the way our church building has a dynamism of its own. The environment of our church has spoken to us and to many people over the years. People have found strength in times of personal trouble, insight in times of confusion, and gratitude in times of blessings. We want our church to continue to be a spiritual home and haven for generations to come, for our children and their children.

Our response solidifies with a spiritual realization — everything we have is a gift from God. When we generously give back to God, God will bless us in return. Generosity is a virtue. Generosity is a statement of our desire to participate in God's work, to bring God into the lives of people far and near. Generosity is a statement of trust...we believe that when we give with a bold spirit and give more than a conservative amount, God will insure that we continue to live with happiness, joy, and financial stability.

I realize that in the Catholic community of Lexington there are other capital campaigns taking place. We pray for the success of every campaign which is seeking to develop the ministry of our Church and I trust that we can all be successful. But this success will call for strong participation by EVERYONE within our community. We can do it...the key is having a vision and giving with faith.

As St. Francis was dedicating his life to Jesus, he heard Jesus say, "Francis, rebuild my Church. "For a period of time, Francis and his friends engaged in the physical labor of repairing some dilapidated churches. Then the Lord told him again, "No not that; rebuild the spirit of the Church." In many ways, that story is relevant for us. We are not just about fund-raising and repairs, but also about deepening the spirit of all of us — so that we generously and eagerly desire to go deep and therefore repair and renew our spiritual home!

An important theme in the Church is to focus more on our mission than on maintenance. At first it may seem to be a contradiction that we are putting so much energy into a campaign related to our Church's maintenance. However, in order to fulfill our mission, we need our parish headquarters to be a place that invites us to hear, respond to and then share the Good News of Christ Our King. I invite you to invest in our mission by investing in our Capital Campaign. Our Capital Campaign will culminate in 2020, the 75th anniversary of the founding of our parish. I invite you to help prepare our parish for the next 75 years. ♛

Wow!!!! As a congregation our response to the mid-June Mission Appeal by Father Tom Carroll for support for the Piarist High School in Eastern Kentucky was very strong. Based just on that first weekend, the $17,000+ collected exceeded by $5000 the highest response in recent years we have made to a Mission Appeal. Thank you!!!

I believe that there are some messages which this response gives.

A congregation like ours responds to a clear, impassioned and inspiring message. Fr. Tom certainly offered that; his physical presence and faith-filled determination spoke volumes.

Secondly, our response signals that we have taken one step further to embrace our diocese as a mission diocese, and that we here at our cathedral parish have a unique and powerful ability to help. We are a mission diocese, not only because of the economic, health, and sociological problems that are part of the lives of so many people in Eastern Kentucky, but also because in every county in our diocese, (including Fayette) we Catholics are a distinct minority.

Third, I believe that some of you were predisposed to be especially generous because of some preliminary information. At the beginning of June, our parish magazine, the King's Connection focused on Eastern Kentucky. Also the bulletin and our "electronic news blasts" alerted you to the up-coming second collection and its purpose. (I make a Mission Appeal for our diocese somewhere around the country on an annual basis...there have been times when I arrived at a parish to make such an appeal, and the only people knowing that I was coming were the pastor and his secretary!)

Some of you gave as instant givers...but many of you came prepared to go deep, you were intentional givers.

I observed the same phenomenon at the recent fund-raiser for Catholic Charities. A lot of energy was expended to generate an enthusiastic response. And so the crowd was larger than usual and the money raised for this wonderful ministry was more than has been raised in recent years by the same event.

Throughout the Church, this weekend marks the close of our fiscal year and the beginning of the next fiscal year. It will take a few weeks to close our books and to give a report on 2017-2018. However as we enter 2018-2019 I lift up the importance of a dedication to intentional giving. This involves having a plan for giving, a schedule for giving, and such a commitment that, when there is a monthly amount budgeted for the Church and other charities, that donation is always the first one made. Such an approach has a strong spiritual component, and is basically an investment in the ministry of the Church and an expression of trust in God.

As we enter 2018-2019, our Capital Campaign is like a basketball team entering the fourth quarter, and victory is in sight, but not guaranteed. We have the goal that everyone on the team will make a contribution. Also in October, our Diocesan Annual appeal will take place. Primary beneficiaries of the money generated by the appeal are our Appalachian parishes and Catholic Charities. We generally have only about 30 percent of our parishioners contribute to this. We need to increase that number of participants. Additionally, we need to grow our offertory collections for our parish. I have suggested adding $10 per week, or starting with $10 per week if you are not contributing. Thanks to all who have positively responded.

We are the flagship among the parishes in our diocese. Our challenge is to open our minds and hearts to see how our financial gifts enhance the mission of the Diocese and our parish. Once we have those needs emblazoned on our hearts, we are ready to take the next step as intentional givers. ♛

A s we prepare to enter the month of October, I ask you to prayerfully consider the kind of generosity and organization which will enable you to support the work of the Church on three levels.

We need to be stronger in our Sunday collections, our Capital Campaign is entering a critical stretch run, and October is also the month of our Diocesan Annual Appeal.

As we prayerfully reflect on our parish's day by day operating expenses, I refer you to our Parish Mission statement.

*We are a parish dedicated to living and spreading the power of the Eucharist and the joy of the Gospel. We are dedicated to parish-wide formation as intentional disciples so that all will be equipped to fulfill Christ's Great Commission to our home, Church, and world. "Go therefore and make disciples of all nations, baptizing them in the name of the Father, and the Son, and the Holy Spirit, teaching them to observe all that I have commanded you" — MATTHEW 28:19-20*

As we prayerfully reflect on our Capital Campaign, I refer to our Campaign Prayer.

Dear Lord, we dedicate our Capital Campaign to your glory. We thank you for the blessings you have given us through our Church. We have encountered you and many good people here in our spiritual home. Within the walls of our buildings we have found direction for our lives, strength in times of weakness, and perspective in times of success. We humbly ask you to bless our campaign to prepare our cathedral parish to be a home and a haven for years to come. Open our hearts to be guided by the prayers of Mary and the many saintly people who have been part of the life of this parish. Send your Holy Spirit to inspire us as we participate in our campaign to stabilize our church facilities. Bless us so that we can turn this challenge into an opportunity to trust and praise you.

As we prayerfully reflect on our response to the Appeal on behalf of the needs of our mission diocese we can pray with an adaptation of the prayer of the 25th Anniversary of our Diocese (2013).

Almighty God, through the ages you watch over your daughters and sons. Ever-faithful, you call us to respond to your grace. As we celebrate 30 years of mission as the Diocese of Lexington, we humbly ask you to deepen our faith, fill our hearts with your love, strengthen our encounter with Christ in the Eucharist; guide us as one family, embolden us to proclaim the Gospel; and help us to open the door of faith to all we meet. Grant this through our Lord Jesus Christ, your Son who lives and reigns with you in the unity of the Holy Spirit, one God, for ever and ever. Amen. ♛

ONE IN CHRIST

Next weekend, the cards for the Giving Tree will be all around the inside walls of our Church. They serve as invitations for our generosity for the people within our community who are in need. Some of the cards invite us to buy specific gifts...some are asking for financial donations. If the pattern holds true, there will be a great deal of energy in our Church after each of our Masses next weekend, as people go from card to card and make some decisions on how to be of assistance. There is a particular joy at the prospect of giving and bringing some joy to the lives of families and brothers and sisters who are on the edge.

The months of November and December are special times for giving...and for seeking support. The spirits of Thanksgiving and Christmas, plus the strategy of year-end giving are all part of this milieu. We receive many solicitations in the mail from worthy causes. Some of them are from organizations and causes which we personally have supported for many years; some come from organizations which seem to have gotten our names from some surreptitious list.

Concurrently, we do have some very important causes here at home. We here at Christ the King are entering the third and critical year of our Capital Campaign...we are doing fairly well, but we have not met our goal yet. We are called to support the many ministries throughout our missionary diocese by our donations and pledges to the Diocesan Annual Appeal. And we are running behind budget on our offertory collections. These are all critical issues.

How do we find it within ourselves to respond? There is an entire field of business related to charitable giving...but I will offer three tips which are important to me...

Have a vision...seek to see the lives that will be changed by the ministry throughout our missionary diocese and in our community and the larger world...see in our hearts the healing, the new leases on life, the hope that people can receive...envision the stability and efficiency of our building as it welcomes so many people in so many different situations of need...have a picture of all we can do here as we balance our budget and continue to develop programs that serve you, your family and our community....When we have a vision, giving is motivated by a sense of mission.

Do financial planning...many do this planning from a spirit of tithing...giving 5 percent of income to the work of the Church and 5 percent of income to other charities... this also means trusting that 90 percent of your income will provide a good life and the necessary savings for you and your household.

Trust that God will give you a special joy and peace as you give, as you trust, and as you see the good work of the Church and other charities you support. There is a joy in giving, as we place ourselves in the hands of God a bit more than usual, as we invest in the lives of brothers and sisters and thereby expand our zone of compassion and love, and as we free ourselves from some of our personal spirit of consumerism and the hyper-quest for security which is financially based. ♛

# CHAPTER 38

## *A Response to Victims of Abuse by Priests:*

BULLETIN — September 16, 2018

Throughout the world, and certainly throughout America, we Catholics have been overwhelmed with the revelation of the extent of sexual abuse by priests and the attendant mismanagement and cover-up of these criminal and evil deeds. Church leaders are seeking to respond with justice, compassion, and also with prayer and penance. As soon as we could, we hosted a listening session here at Christ the King. We priests and deacons have preached about it and Bishop John has written a pastoral letter to all within our diocese. It has been a topic we have dealt with in many other settings, in meetings, classes and in informal discussions.

The priests of the eight Lexington parishes which comprise the Fayette Deanery are meetings every Tuesday morning, at an early hour, in order to pray together and to develop a Deanery-wide response of pastoral care. This week we will be having a Deanery meeting to clarify our pastoral plan. This past week, there was a meeting scheduled to bring priests together to pray for vocations and to consider ways to recruit for the priesthood. The content of that meeting needed to be changed to give the opportunity for priests to de-brief, to pray, and to articulate that recruitment for the priesthood has taken on a new dimension.

In the midst of the flood of feelings that run a very wide range, listening to those who are hurt is more important than explaining how extensively abuse runs through our society, how the cover-ups could have occurred, or how the problems reached the extent they did in a way of life so respected. Listening is even more important than outlining the lessons learned, the protective policies instituted over the past 15 years, and mapping out a response to the revelations of abuse and cover-ups.

> 66
>
> *Listening is even more important than outlining the lessons learned, the protective policies instituted over the past 15 years, and mapping out a response to the revelations of abuse and cover-ups.*
>
> 99

Listening...with a readiness to hear the unexpected...listening...with a willingness to be vulnerable...listening...with a desire to be guided by what we hear...listening...with an openness to be moved to tears...listening...as we believe Jesus is listening...listening...as we honor and reverence the range of experiences and feelings...listening some more when we feel we have done it enough...listening...with our hearts...listening...as we trust that what we hear will lead to the right kind of actions...listening...as we let go of a need to be in control...listening...to the messiness of feelings...listening...and allowing the words we hear to be scriptural and evocative of prayer.

We are ready to listen...our pastoral staff is ready to listen...I am ready to listen...please contact me if you need to talk. ♛

# CHAPTER 39

*Our Church Steeple:*

BULLETIN — September 13, 2020

Cincinnati is a city built on seven hills. One of the hills, Mt. Adams, has several high overlooks where you can see the meandering Ohio River and across the river, my hometown, Bellevue, Ky. Often when I am looking across the river to Bellevue I am flooded with many memories. From that vantage point I have never been able to see the house in which I grew up. But Sacred Heart Church, my home parish, always stands out. The steeple and bell tower are the first noticeable aspects of the church.

A church steeple points to the heavens and to the One who is beyond the heavens. It also reminds us that God desires to come down to where we are. The church steeple helps people find the church as they are searching for a place to pray, to feel solace, to encounter God. A church steeple adds elegance to an edifice which tends to be functional. The church steeple suggests that there is more to life than what we know from our place on the ground. Steeples on Catholic churches usually have a crucifix at the top, as this symbol of Jesus' love and sacrifice inspires gratitude and encourages us to live our lives with a spirit of love and a readiness to sacrifice .

A church bell sometimes chimes out the time, but always is a call to prayer, to attentiveness to God's work in our daily lives and our responsibility to pray and to share in God's work through the day. The bell seems to say, "Be alert. God is near." It is always good to rejoice with the beauty and power of the church bell as it peals at various times and for various occasions.

For the next two weeks or so, beginning on Monday, our church steeple will be replaced and our church bell will be refurbished and its capability expanded. We are excited by the prospect of watching this major project move along step by step. We have made some temporary adjustments to our Mass location, schedule and entry points in order to accommodate the work that will be transpiring. Both the company

*Photo by Maureen Guarnieri-Yeager*

working with our steeple (from Campbellsville, Ky.) and the company working with our bell (from Cincinnati) have strong reputations and a spirit of ministry as they serve churches nationwide. Let's keep in our prayers the safety of all the personnel who will be involved in the projects.

As always, I am grateful to our facility and maintenance staff and their team of volunteers for their wonderful work in coordinating these projects. And thanks need to be directed to all of you who have contributed to our capital campaign .

This weekend, we are beginning a four-weekend series of First Communion Masses for the children who were unable to make their First Communions in the spring. These Masses will be private for the children and their families and will be guided by our safety protocol. I thank the ushers and music ministers who will be helping to insure that these Masses will be safe and memorable celebrations.

This weekend was scheduled to be the time for Oktoberfest. I thank the chair couples who are in the midst of planning a virtual Oktoberfest. I encourage everyone to keep up the Oktoberfest spirit, to consider toasting life with an Oktoberfest-type beverage and to plan to be part of the Oktoberdash and the Oktoberfest raffle. We can still turn this modified Oktoberfest into a great gift for our parish and school. Let's do it together! ⛏

# CHAPTER 40

*Marriage:*

BULLETIN — June 3, 2018

BULLETIN — October 7, 2018

L ast weekend our Cathedral was the location for five different Wedding Masses. One was Friday evening, one was Sunday afternoon and the others were on Saturday morning, afternoon and evening. (Five different priests celebrated a wedding here that weekend.) I guess you could say that was a strong kickoff to the wedding season.

Couples very often express their appreciation for the extensive marriage preparation that the Catholic Church offers. This is not "red tape", but is a gift to the couple, helping them to be sure, to realize and work on any issues which can become problematic, and to give thanks to God for the call they have received to enter this vocation of Matrimony. It is good that this preparation process begins at least six months before the wedding date.

Each member of the engaged couple takes a pre-marriage inventory called FOCCUS. FOCCUS has been designed by a team of psychologists, marriage experts, and pastoral ministers. It consists of over a hundred statements to which each person must mark agree, disagree, or unsure. If either member of the couple is unsure about an item or if either or both disagree with the ideal answer, then that item is a topic for discussion. This is not a pass/fail test, but does provide a good indication of areas where a couple need to communicate further. The items are classified into topics such as communication, problem-solving, lifestyle expectations, personality match, religion, spirituality and values, sexuality, extended family, readiness for marriage, friends and interests, dual careers, understanding of the covenant of marriage, financial issues and readiness issues. It also has sections for couples to fill out when they are interfaith, cohabiting, or if one or both have children already, or this is not the first marriage for one or both. FOCCUS is taken online, scored by a professional group, and then the priest or deacon working with the couple discusses the results with the couple in one or more meetings.

There are also two marriage preparation seminars the couple is required to participate in, one on the spirituality of marriage (based on the *Theology of the Body*) and one which reviews many of the basics of a healthy marriage. These seminars are led by trained facilitators and there are more than a dozen couples in attendance. There are presentations, practical advice and discussions, plus times for each engaged couple to talk as a couple. These two elements can also be handled within the Diocesan Pre-Marriage Retreat at Cliffview. There are also alternate possibilities of a couple meeting with a parish-designated sponsor couple or participating in an Engaged Encounter. Additionally, whether in a seminar or by taking an online class, the Church calls for couples to learn about Natural Family Planning.

In the midst of all this, the couple works with the priest or deacon guiding their preparation process to do some documentation and formally verify that they are getting married with the right spirit and intentions. Meanwhile, of course, there are preparations for the wedding and the reception; but even more so for the Liturgy and for the music, songs, scripture readings, and the flow of the special parts of the wedding liturgy.

I always suggest to a couple that they can trust that at their wedding there will be some folks who are struggling with some kind of love relationship, and that what we do and how we do it can be a gift to those who come with their own needs of the heart. So, even on their wedding day, a couple can evangelize as they enter into the vocation of marriage. ♛

One of the most enjoyable of the Diocesan Masses which takes place here at our cathedral is the annual Wedding Anniversary Mass which we celebrate at this Saturday's 5 p.m. Mass. Married couples from throughout our diocese come here to celebrate benchmark anniversaries. Some couples come every year because it is a wonderful time of prayer and a beautiful affirmation of the Sacrament of Matrimony. Welcome, we are glad you are here!

Those involved in marriage enrichment speak of five stages of marriage. There is the honeymoon stage, where all is romantic and ideal. There is the stage of disillusion, when there is the realization that not all is as perfect as once was thought or hoped. There is the stage of misery, "How in the world did I get married to this person who drives me nuts." Then there is the evaluative stage, where the pluses and strengths are seen clearly and there is the realization that the strengths far outweigh the problems (and there is a mutual commitment to work through the problems). Then there is the mature and maturing stage, where the couple go deeper into their union and develop a shared sense of mission.

Marriage works best when the husband and wife are best friends. Together they are called to generate new life, often by having children and guiding them into true Christian lives. In a good marriage, the husband and wife draw the best out of one another. The love they have for one another, the trust they have in one another, and the comfort in one another's arms offers a window into the love that God has for them. A good wife and husband help one another to clarify and refine their ideals, to rebound from life's disappointments, and to stay true to their principles.

The vocation of marriage has a way of deepening as the years move on. Ultimately, each person helps the other to get to heaven. But during all the years of marriage, a Christian husband and wife encourage and support one another in their works of charity, service and compassion.

In the famous passage of St. Paul in his First Epistle to the Corinthians, he states that love is the most important gift of all. Love is kind, patient, courteous, forgiving, honest, other-centered and humble…And yet, love is a choice, a decision, because for most of us, love is not simple and second-nature. We need to be dedicated to make the decision to give the gift of love.

Family life is full of joys and challenges. It is the Domestic Church. Marriage and family life are the schools where we learn to Respect Life. As we observe Respect Life Sunday, I invite you to give thanks for the wholesome Christian families who have impacted your lives and have taught you by word and example about the sanctity of life. ♛

Wedding Anniversary Celebration

# CHAPTER 41

*Mercy:*

BULLETIN — April 8, 2018

BULLETIN — April 19, 2020

As we celebrate Divine Mercy Sunday we give thanks for all the blessings of our Lenten and Easter Liturgical and Spiritual celebrations. On behalf of all of us, I express appreciation to our choirs, our liturgy committee members, all our liturgical ministers, and to Bishop John for the special gifts he brings. Now as we celebrate Divine Mercy Sunday, we focus on the great gift of Jesus being with us in the Blessed Sacrament. We celebrate also the great gift of the Sacrament of Penance. (On Good Friday afternoon, five of us priests heard confessions in church non-stop for a total of 15 hours!) The Sacrament of Penance is one of the most powerful expressions of the Divine Mercy of Jesus. Divine Mercy Sunday reminds us that Jesus had mercy on a broken world and so became incarnate and gave his life for us. In the post-resurrection readings, I am always struck by the narrative in John's Gospel of the mercy that Jesus had on St. Peter.

On this weekend we are challenged to re-invest ourselves in the spirit of mercy and to live as disciples of Jesus who do the works of mercy. I thank you for the generous support of our special collections, support which speaks of the mercy you have for victims of disasters and injustices throughout the world.

In the midst of the many instances of school violence that have rocked our nation, let us have mercy on those with mental illness, compassion on those whose grief is so acute that they are overwhelmed with anger, mercy on those so fearful that they demand 100 percent assurance of their loved ones' safety, and mercy on those who make mistakes or fall short of doing what is needed to prevent violence.

Let us do the works of mercy as we care for the sick, the dying, the poor, the homeless, refugees and immigrants, prisoners, those addicted, and those who for one reason or another feel defeated by life's misfortunes.

Let us have mercy on those who are spiritually lost, confused or so insecure that they fall into self-righteousness. Let us have a special place in our hearts for those whom we have a difficult time forgiving. Let us reach out to those who are searching for truth. Let us pray for the right time and words to challenge those who are living lives of self-destruction and hurtfulness. Let us trust the power of prayer, trust the power of advocacy, trust the power of wise decisions, and trust the power of mercy.

Finally, on Divine Mercy Sunday, I thank all of you who have had mercy on me. I know I have made some mistakes as rector. I know that there are some times when my own sins and imperfections can get in the way of listening, speaking or acting as you need me to respond. Thank you for your mercy...God is not finished with me yet. ◢

Every day during the Governor's briefing, we are encouraged to sacrifice. We are encouraged to let go of some aspects of our daily lives that are part of our daily joy. We are entitled to gather with friends, to gather for worship, to be close to our friends, to enjoy leisurely shopping, to go into our place of work...but we need to refrain from those kinds of behaviors...to make a sacrifice, so that we and others can be safe.

The two Latin words which are blended to form the word "sacrifice" are "sacrum" — "holy" and "facio" — " to make"...to sacrifice is to make holy.

In the history of religion, sacrifices were made as expressions of faith. Something or someone valuable was relinquished, or even destroyed with a raw sense of trust that God would provide even more blessings and even more of the truly good life. Whether that sacrifice was the first fruits of the field, 10 percent of one's income, or the Son of God, sacrifices have made people more holy throughout the centuries.

Our sacrifices during Lent have had the intention of helping us conquer our temptations, to avoid sin, and to get closer and closer to holiness, or to become the whole person that God intends us to be as we have been made in God's image. The sacrifices an athlete makes are part and parcel of attaining the joy of peak performance. Parents make sacrifices for

> *We give thanks for the mercy Jesus has had on our broken world and our broken lives, and we trust that there is more mercy to come.*

their children so that the children can fulfill their potential. As we see our sacrifices make a difference, the sacrifice becomes less painful and a source of joy.

The pandemic has hurled us into a unique environment of sacrifice. Members of every human community are being called to make the same sacrifices. There is a special bond, a kind of holiness, in the shared commitment and solidarity. Hopefully, our sacrifices being made today will not only keep us and our world safe, but will also lead to a re-evaluation of what is most important in our lives and will lead us to a more integrated sense of closeness and intimacy with those whom we love, including our God. For us as Christians, we are able to sustain our commitment to sacrifice by the power of our prayers and our vision of the results.

This is Divine Mercy Sunday. We give thanks for the mercy Jesus has had on our broken world and our broken lives, and we trust that there is more mercy to come. We gratefully pray in the spirit of the French phrase, "merci beaucoup". Mercy implies that Jesus helps us to heal and that Jesus has sacrificed himself to give us a new lease on life, a deeper relationship with God, and a stronger actualization of our true self. Our Eucharist continues the sacrifice, as Jesus gives himself to us in the consecrated bread and wine which are transfigured into his Body and Blood.

In many ways, as we sacrifice in response to the pandemic, we contribute to the holiness of our world and predispose ourselves to trust the power of sacrifices. "There is a time for everything...a time to embrace, and a time to be far from embraces..."
— ECCLESIASTES 3:5.

# CHAPTER 42

## The Quest for Racial Equality:

BULLETIN — January 14, 2018

BULLETIN — September 22, 2019

BULLETIN — August 2, 2020

This Monday we observe Martin Luther King Day. As we reflect on his life, his ministry, and the social issues he addressed, several points stand out.

Our nation has made progress in the quest for racial justice, a fair treatment of all people, and the conviction that all people are members of God's family, no matter what our race, creed or color. But as instances of racial injustice and violence and subsequent riots bear witness, we still have a long way to go.

Many of the principles of Martin Luther King's leadership continue to offer sound guidance as we seek to move forward.

Prayer is at the heart of the work of a Christian to bring about a just change. It is faith that the will of God is for justice. It is faith that justice will eventually prevail. Prayer girds us to stay with the principles we wish to follow.

The style of Martin Luther King's campaign for racial justice was non-violence. Non-violence calls for humility, courage, and constant prayer and solidarity. Non-violence needs to be more than a strategy, but a way of life. It seeks to educate and change people, to bring about understanding and mutual respect. Non-violence seeks to defeat injustice, not people.

Non-violence trusts that there is often some suffering which results from taking a stand or participating in a demonstration, but also knows that such suffering can educate, transform and convert those who inflict the suffering.

Non-violence chooses love, not hate. There is the realization that a prejudiced person is a victim more so than he or she is a person who is intrinsically evil. Non-violent love is an active love, not a passive love. Non-violent love does not simply want to win, but wants what is best for everyone, even for those who have been hurtful. The goal of Martin Luther King's non-violent campaign was reconciliation and redemption.

Coalitions are important. The image of Dr. King and leaders of various religious groups marching together is powerful. The witness of sports and entertainment figures is important. The leadership which our Church can offer is essential.

The quest for justice calls for some level of scholarly work. Dr. King studied Gandhi. St. Francis is a model of working for peace and respect. Mother Teresa's goal was to do daily what is right and she then left the results in God's hands. Even today, we do well to study the life and teachings of Martin Luther King and other activists for peace and justice.

Martin Luther King Day serves as reminder that we are all brothers and sisters and that if we work together, we can tear down the barriers which divide us. On this day, I hope we can all sing in our hearts…"We shall overcome, I do believe, we'll walk hand in hand, we shall overcome…some day."

On Monday evenings till early November, I am going to Cincinnati to attend a continuing education course at the archdiocesan seminary, the Athenaeum of Ohio. The course is entitled, "The Church and the Civil War." There are ten two hour classes; we have had three so far. It is an interesting course for one like me who is a moderate civil war buff; but it also offers some points which are relevant for our culture and our Church today.

As our class has considered slavery, the lack of a clear teaching stands out. In 1839, Pope Gregory XVI forbade Trans-Atlantic slave trade, but did not forbid slavery or the slave trade within a nation. In the antebellum years, some clergy and religious had slaves; and even a few motherhouses of sisters did so. At the time the war was breaking out, many U.S. Catholic Church leaders felt that slavery was a political issue in which they should not get involved. (The Catholic Church in the U.S. was made up of many recent immigrants who had been targets of prejudice upon their arrival; it seemed expedient for many Catholics to prove their patriotism and allegiance to their new homeland by accepting the national policy...plus there was the concern that freed slaves would compete with recent immigrants for jobs.) Along the Ohio River, Bishop Purcell of Cincinnati was a strong abolitionist and supporter of the Union cause, whereas, Louisville's Bishop Spalding advocated for peace and the gradual emancipation of slaves. In most instances, Catholic Church leaders did not take an active leadership role.

Since then, the U.S. Church has been taking a much stronger stance on moral issues. The Church has been an advocate for just labor laws, for peace and nuclear disarmament, and certainly for the right to life of the unborn. Currently, we are being encouraged by our nation's bishops and other Catholic leaders to work for an approach to immigration which offers a compassionate understanding of the terrible situations from which immigrants are fleeing and their desire to begin a new life in the U.S.

Beginning today and continuing till next weekend, there are cards at the entrances to Church on which you can offer your support to the Kentucky Bishops' advocacy to our legislators so that our legislators will champion a policy which is more welcoming to immigrants from chaotic, impoverished, and violent homelands.

The issue of immigration is not a simple issue, it calls for significant study and dialogue; but it is an over-statement to describe the majority of the immigrants, whether documented or undocumented, as criminals or threats. I realize there needs to be limits; I do not have any answers; but I do know our nation is a nation of immigrants, with a strong spirit of welcoming, and that there are many immigrants who have come from situations where their lives and the lives of their family members are in danger. So I encourage you to sign cards and put them in the basket at our Church doors...and to pray, study and work for a just and Christ-centered resolution of this crisis. The deadline for our collection of cards is next Sunday, September 29, World Day of Migrants and Refugees. ♛

Change is in the air. Demonstrations have been taking place; there is the realization that for some time black lives have mattered less to white people than white lives; Confederate statues are removed; buildings and public areas are being renamed; language is being refine; kneeling ballplayers are regarded as prophetic; and history is being re-written to name some ugly truths.

Many of us who are white would say that we are not prejudiced. And yet many of us have not taken to heart the experiences of racial prejudice which have been the lot of African Americans.

I know that I do not have much contact with African Americans who have been impacted by racism.

The starting point for being an ally in the quest to end racism is to understand or "stand under" the experience of others. Study, participation in discussion groups, and working together for social change offer great opportunities for listening, learning and moving forward together. Very often, sports, school, and work provide opportunities for understanding, and yet, often there are limits to how much we are able to see one another's world.

I am grateful for the prayer service we had on June 22, that was described as and has served as a first step for our parish to do our part to alleviate racism. Meg Campos has led virtual discussion groups on the United States Catholic Bishops' Pastoral Letter on Racism entitled "Open Wide Our Hearts." Several leaders have stepped forward to continue the momentum and will lead different initiatives related to on-going learning, building bridges between communities and advocacy efforts. We plan to name a new outreach ministry that will house these efforts. Our hope is to provide an avenue that can connect us all in some way with the African-American experience — no matter where we are in the process.

In Lexington, there is a faith-based advocacy group B.U.I.L.D. Over 25 congregations are members of B.U.I.L.D. Most of Lexington's Catholic Churches are members and so too are several African American congregations. The purpose of B.U.I.L.D. is to work for justice and to influence the changing of policies, practices and budgets so that Lexington can be a safer community. Lexington's issues are a responsibility for all of us, whether or not our own neighborhoods are primarily affected.

Over the course of a year, B.U.I.L.D. leaders conduct research, host listening sessions, determine the key issues to address, develop a consensus, have rallies, and culminate this process with an action meeting where city officials and decision-makers are challenged to make the changes which B.U.I.L.D. has determined will be helpful for the safety and progress of all. All this is done in a prayerful context, grounded in scripture study.

This past year the key areas of B.U.I.L.D.'s advocacy have been addressing issues of violence and shootings in Lexington neighborhoods, mental health issues, drugs, affordable housing, and racial issues in our city schools.

These are not solely African-American issues, but many of those who are victims and who live in fear and uncertainty are African-Americans. Additionally, participation in B.U.I.L.D. provides one of the rare opportunities most of us will have to work together with and grow in our understanding of the Black person's experience.

Christ the King's history with B.U.I.L.D. is that we occasionally get a fair amount of people to come to Heritage Hall in the spring for the action meeting, but because they have not been part of the process all through the year, they are confused and do not stay with B.U.I.L.D.

When we begin our B.U.I.L.D. season in the fall, please consider being part of the process from the get-go. You can help change occur and you can meet some great people and grow in your understanding of the African-American experience. ♛

# CHAPTER 43

## *Halloween, All Saints and Souls:*

BULLETIN — October 28, 2018

Our hearts are restless, till they rest in Thee". This is a classic line from one of the prayers of St. Augustine. This week, in a heart-felt manner, we enter into the mysteries of eternal life and the very human emotions of grief, hope and joy.

On Thursday, we celebrate the feast of All Saints. It is a holy day of obligation. We all are encouraged to give thanks for the many people among our friends, family, and heroes who have touched our lives, who have concluded their years on earth, and who now rest in eternal glory. They have not been formally canonized as saints but they are reaping the rewards of their good lives. The way they lived their lives on earth set the stage for their unity with God and the angels and saints in the mystery of heaven. Their souls are resting in peace.

Friday, All Souls' Day is a day when our 5:30 p.m. Mass is particularly dedicated to the memory of those whose funerals took place here over the past year. Our Bereavement Committee offers a special time of prayer and remembrance in a supportive environment by means of the Mass and the subsequent reception. All Souls' Day traditionally has a spirit of intercessory prayer...if a deceased person is still needing something in the way of purgation, or needs to go deeper in their desire and love for God, our prayers can offer a needed boost. All Souls' Day reminds us that God's mercy is very great, and that if a person dies with a sense of incompleteness, our prayers help them to open their eyes, their hearts and their souls to the Divine Intimacy which God offers so generously. "May the souls of the faithful departed rest in peace."

Wednesday is Halloween, a day that has taken on a different character since its sacred origin as the Vigil of All Saints Day. Children of all ages love to wear a costume, to look like someone or something different than their present self, to delight in scaring others or being scared, and to restlessly prowl neighborhoods, seeking treats which are outside the realm of a healthy diet. Halloween can be extensively analyzed as a strange social phenomenon, or simply enjoyed. I suggest that we celebrate the fun even as we realize that our restless hearts do wonder who we will be as life goes on, who we might have been if life would have presented other challenges and opportunities, and who we are as we balance our craving for treats in a world where we can be complicit in the trickiness of evil. "Our hearts are restless till they rest in Thee."

We give thanks for our school's seventh grade students who will enhance our All Saints Day Mass as they emulate many particular saints, we give thanks to our Bereavement committee for the special gift they offer on All Souls' Day, and we give thanks for the children of Halloween, who remind us to not take ourselves too seriously. ♛

# CHAPTER 44

*Thanksgiving:*

BULLETIN — November 27, 2016

BULLETIN — November 18, 2018

BULLETIN — November 24, 2019

BULLETIN — November 22, 2020

Today as we begin our Advent season, we are fortified by the energy of our celebration of Thanksgiving Day. Thanksgiving can usher in a hectic season of parties and shopping, but it can also serve as a stimulus to our contemplative spirit. We all have much for which we can be grateful. We have the blessings of families, friends, work, health, many accomplishments and savored memories. But we also have the blessings of faith, hope and love.

Even though some of us have not had an externally "great year", there are still solid grounds for gratitude. Thanksgiving might present a challenge to see the good in the midst of the bad and the ugly, but faith, hope and love open our eyes to see the blessings we have experienced and the blessings we have facilitated.

Thanksgiving Day also reminds us that we are pilgrims, and we are called to be a people who welcome pilgrims. We are pilgrims because our lives are like one grand pilgrimage as we journey towards unity with God and the fulfillment of our lives in heaven. We are all looking for God, for God's love and for a clear experience of God.

> *Advent is a pilgrimage in several ways. This season reminds us of the never-ending human yearning to feel the love of God. Advent prepares us to accompany Joseph and Mary as they make their pilgrimage to Bethlehem and its holy manger.*

We are also like hosts and guides for fellow pilgrims. We sometimes give of our resources, our time and our very selves to immigrants and refugees. We need to remind ourselves that we are descendants of refugees and immigrants. We need to encourage fellow pilgrims that their journey is worthwhile and that they will give new insights and energy to our culture.

For any pilgrim...whether seeking a new homeland or seeking the fullness of our spiritual home...there is often a critical point of LIMINALITY, where we feel lost, without direction or hope, overwhelmed by uncertainty. The Advent season reminds us that such times are most conducive for us to open our eyes and notice the love and power of God.

Advent is a pilgrimage in several ways. This season reminds us of the never-ending human yearning to feel the love of God. Advent prepares us to accompany Joseph and Mary as they make their pilgrimage to Bethlehem and its holy manger. Advent prepares us to welcome Jesus into our hearts as we make our own pilgrimage to encounter our new-born King.

May the contemplative moments of Thanksgiving Day set the stage for special contemplative times during our Advent pilgrimage. ♛

Pope Francis has called for this Sunday to be a World Day of Prayer for those who are poor. Many people throughout the world live without enough to eat, with no roof over their heads, with no income, sub-standard health care, and they very often live with constant violence and with little hope. This week, which leads into Thanksgiving, is also a time of particular sensitivity to those who are struggling in poverty. We are very grateful for the food drives and the special meals which are offered to the poor, and we are grateful for the agencies which provide charitable and empowering services to those who are impoverished. We who are blessed need to make sure that our generosity at this time of the year is a springboard to our willingness to go deeper as we seek to help brothers and sisters improve their lives.

Thanksgiving calls to mind the vulnerability of both the first pilgrims and the Native Americans who welcomed them as they celebrated a feast together, sharing food and sharing their common humanity. That first thanksgiving was not predictive of the ways our migrating ancestors would treat the people who lived here before they crossed the ocean.

The original national holiday of Thanksgiving dates from President Lincoln's desire to bring some hope to an internally embattled nation on the verge of implosion. Thanksgiving is not a simple, uncomplicated day. It is a day of feasting, reunions, and reflections... but it can also be a day of excesses, disagreements and disappointments.

Thanksgiving can be a day when we treat the poor as if they were rich...but maybe it is a more true thanksgiving when we who are rich realize that we are also poor. The First Beatitude in Luke's Gospel says "blessed are the poor". Blessed are those who know how much they need God; blessed are those who have strong grounds for thanksgiving, blessed are those who realize that everything they have is a gift from God . The rich person, obsessed with the quest for more riches and material security, is really quite impoverished and trapped.

In the Gospel of Matthew, the first Beatitude is "Blessed are the Poor in Spirit". Blessed are those who are humble, who are not afraid to pick up the odor of the sheep, who are willing to be vulnerable, who know who they and who they are not, who trust in God, who seek to be the hands of Jesus.

The beginning of the 12-step creed echoes the concept of poverty of spirit: admitting powerlessness and trusting that only the Supreme Being can overcome the addiction. The Jewish people in the desert, guided by Moses, eventually realized how much they needed God in order to arrive in the Promised Land. The repentant sinner, desiring healing, knows the need for God.

My Thanksgiving prayer is that we not focus on all that we have, but on how we are brothers and sisters with the poor, that we focus on what our poverty teaches us, and that we pray for the courage and insight to find ways to help life be better for those who are living on the edge. ♛

Last weekend, Fr. Damian, Deacon Paul and I were part of a packed house as the Habitat for Humanity home of Asende and Sera and their family was dedicated and blessed. Asende was a regular member of the team of volunteers who built the house. He and Sera are natives of the Congo. It was a celebration of great joy, hope and community. Habitat for Humanity is a wonderful organization which has built thousands of homes throughout the world, for (and with!) people who could not build or finance the house on their own. Every year, for 30 years, the eight Catholic parishes of Lexington have band together and provide financial sponsorship and volunteers for the construction of a Habitat for Humanity home. A powerful theme on the day of dedication is that the celebration is the dedication of a home more so than a house.

Having a home is important to all of us. This week many of us will have a meal and share words of gratitude, encouragement and love as we gather in our homes and the homes of friends and loved ones to celebrate Thanksgiving. Home is the place where religion is taught by example more so than by words, where the importance of faith is a cornerstone, and where prayer and a sense of God's presence define the home as the Domestic Church. Out homes are where we express ourselves in so many ways, but also where we find our true selves, and where we know we can be our true selves and work our way through clumsy and confusing stages as we grow into the people God has made us to be.

When the televised news shows homes destroyed by fires, floods, storms and other natural disasters, our hearts break for the people who have lost their houses, their homes, their history, their hopes, the expression of their family life, creativity and joy.

Our homes are where our hearts are. As we care for refugees and immigrants, we feel their emotions as they grieve the loss of their homes and homeland...and hope for, and struggle mightily, to establish a new home here is our community.

Here at Christ the King, we are in the midst of our Capital Campaign to repair, rehabilitate, and renew our cathedral buildings. In our prayer we "humbly ask God to bless our campaign to prepare our cathedral parish to be a home and a haven for years to come". These are not words written lightly. Many of us have met our best friends here, we have been blessed with forgiveness, understanding, encouragement and great meals. We have shared tears, fears and cheers. We have faced the mysterious workings of our Gracious God and gained some insight, some perspective and greater faith and deepened trust. The very definition of Eucharist encompasses thanksgiving in the context of a community meal.

This is a season of the year when we invite people who have been away from the Church to "come home for Christmas." I encourage you to be part of the team who encourages, invites and welcomes. There is no place like home.

Today as we celebrate the feast of the King for whom our parish is named, we pray that Jesus Christ will be recognized and honored as the King of our hearts, the King of our homes, the King of our diversifying population, the King of our missionary efforts, the King of our world... ♛

As we prepare to celebrate Thanksgiving this weekend, most of us will be doing so with a smaller number of people than usual gathered around the dinner table. And many of us will be in a more intense spirit of reflective prayer than usual. We will have our list of the events and people for which we are grateful. In this column I will offer some of the points that are on my Thanksgiving list.

I am grateful for our increasing spirit of stewardship, which is another way of describing discipleship. Stewardship reminds us of our ability to make a difference by our prayer, our volunteering, and by our financial generosity. Stewardship flows from our willingness to visualize the results of our giving.

Visualizing the results of and visualizing the need for our capital campaign to address the problems in our building's infrastructure has been a big part of our success that has gradually been growing during these years of the campaign, the projects, and the extent of well-planned and well-presented information about the needs and the progress of our projects. I am grateful for the excellent communications which have been a key with this campaign.

I am grateful for our re-furbished bells and our new tower, steeple and cross which provide a majestic visual statement that Christ is the King and that our capital campaign is preparing our parish for the next season of our life.

I am grateful for the generosity which has already been evidenced in our readiness to provide assistance for those in our community and beyond who will be needy as we prepare for winter and continue to journey through our pandemic season.

I am grateful for the pandemic heroes and heroines who are serving in hospitals, nursing homes and prisons and who are stretched and stressed as they continue to give high quality care to those who are victims of the Corona Virus. There is no understating that we are living in a dangerous time and there are many dangerous environments. Please do all you can to keep yourselves and your loved ones safe.

I am grateful on this weekend when we celebrate the 75th anniversary of the founding of our parish for Fr. O'Neill and other visionaries who foresaw the need for a Church and parish complex of our size and who continued to persevere in generating the capital to build.

I am grateful for the ministry of our archives committee which preserves and honors the memory of the development and the spirit of our parish in its founding years. History helps us to know who we are and who we can be as we move forward.

I am grateful for the many ways we have been able to adjust to the pandemic and find ways to minister...I think of the many ways we have prepared our school and school community for in person learning, but also for the creative ways that virtual learning took place in the spring; I am grateful for Zoom and for the approach we have had to the virtual Big Blue Fling and Oktoberfest; I am grateful for our livestreamed Masses which provide an opportunity to pray with our community.

I am grateful for our music ministers, Robert and Gabrielle and the team of cantors, who continue to support us in our sung prayers at Mass.

I am grateful for all the members of our parish and school staff for all the extra ways they are giving of themselves.

And I am grateful for all of you, who continue to keep us in your prayers and who pray for the dire needs of our community, nation and world. Your prayers keep us together, help us to move forward, and strengthen us all as make sacrifices to keep ourselves and others safe. ♛

# CHAPTER 45

## *Advent:*

The feast of St. Nicholas is this Tuesday, December 6. Nicholas is in second place behind the Blessed Virgin Mary as the saint most portrayed in art. St. Nicholas lived in the fourth century. He was born into a wealthy family, but responded to the words of Jesus calling him to sell his goods and give the proceeds to the poor. He lived his life this way.

Eventually, he became the Bishop of Myra, a seaport town in present-day Turkey. Myra is mentioned in the Acts of the Apostles as the harbor where St. Paul and his companions changed ships on one of their missionary journeys. The city of Kale encompasses ancient Myra. A basilica has been built in this city over the tomb of St. Nicholas. Many people come there as pilgrims.

The blend of fact and legend about Nicholas paints an intriguing and endearing picture. Nicholas lived during a time of persecution by the Roman emperor. He was imprisoned at a time when there were so many bishops, priests and deacons in prison that there was not room to incarcerate actual criminals. Upon his release, Nicholas became even more dedicated to care for the poor and downtrodden.

> 66
>
> *Many sweet devotions and warm-hearted practices emerged among Christians in Western Europe about St. Nicholas. Some of them were brought to America by English and Dutch settlers.*
>
> 99

One story maintains that Nicholas made a pilgrimage to the Holy Land, in order to walk in the footsteps of Jesus. Upon his return home, the ship on which he was a passenger was threatened by a ferocious storm. Following the example of Jesus, Nicholas told the storm to be calm...and it did. Nicholas is the patron saint of sailors.

A famous story describes a poor man who had 3 daughters. The man was too poor to provide a dowry for them so that they could get married. The father felt that the only way he could be free of supporting his daughters was for them to become prostitutes. Nicholas saved the girls by three times hurling a bag of gold into the man's home through an open window, so that the girls would each have money for their dowry. Nicholas is the patron of women who are victimized.

A young boy was once kidnapped and made a servant of an evil ruler. Now deceased, Nicholas appeared to the boy, took him home and restored him to his family. Nicholas is also credited with bringing back to life several children who had been killed. Nicholas is the patron of children.

Many sweet devotions and warm-hearted practices emerged among Christians in Western Europe about St. Nicholas. Some of them were brought to America by English and Dutch settlers. Many scholars would say that Santa Claus has some of the same characteristics as St. Nicholas.

At every Sunday and Holyday Mass we pray the Nicene Creed, developed at the Council of Nicea in 325. Nicholas was there, part of the discernment of our core beliefs. Nicholas is also the patron of Greece and Russia, is revered throughout the world and especially on the seas, and is a model for those who seek to protect and care for those are vulnerable and in need of love and encouragement. ♛

W e often live our lives in a different way during this last week before Christmas. Many of us make our last minutes purchases of gifts. We follow the weather reports more closely than usual as we plan some holiday traveling. We have family, neighborhood and office parties; we remind ourselves of the solidarity we have with those who are part of our lives on a regular basis and we open our hearts a bit to those with whom we spend time but do not feel all that connected. We ask the question, "What Mass will we go to on Christmas Eve or Christmas Day?" We decide what we will do, whom we will invite, where we will go on Christmas Eve and Christmas Day. We clarify when we will open presents, we plan menus, and we even evaluate family traditions. But also our hearts are more open than usual to the faith of children, to the revelation of Divine Love which the birth of Jesus offers, and the plight of the poor, sick and lonely at this season of the year.

I think there are three other things we decide this week, however subtly they take place.

We reflect on our lives and how happy and productive we are. We consider what we need to change. We begin to formulate our New Year's Resolution (granted many of us make a resolution to lose weight as we are drinking a second glass of eggnog). But we do some serious self-searching, some soul-exploration as we look at who we are and what we are doing with our lives, and as we implicitly sense that God has made us to be and/or do more. We look at our moral lives, our spiritual lives, our physical lives, our community involvements, our family life and we ask for God's grace to guide and sustain us as we journey forward.

Secondly, this is the season of charitable giving. The Giving Tree and the Christmas Store are powerful examples of our community's generosity. Our hearts are moved as we see people struggling in the cold weather and the coldness of a world that sometimes seems unforgiving. There are many important causes, both locally and beyond. Some of us divide our gift among several causes; some of us have a charity that is dear to us. I encourage you to be extravagantly generous...and to trust that God will give you and your loved ones all you need.

> 66
> *We are a great parish...but like all congregations, we depend on your generosity so that we can continue serving you, our community and our God.*
> 99

Finally, I lift up our cathedral parish of Christ the King. Last weekend we shined at our best as we hosted the Lexington Philharmonic's CATHEDRAL CHRISTMAS to a packed house. On Monday, we hosted the Hispanic Catholic community of Lexington as they celebrated Our Lady of Guadalupe. I am proud of our spirit of prayer, our charitable service, our sense of community, and our education and formation programs. I am proud of our pastoral and school staffs and the many, many volunteers who live out your discipleship. We are a great parish...but like all congregations, we depend on your generosity so that we can continue serving you, our community and our God. Our Christmas offertory collection is very important for our budget. We are in a critical year as parish. I ask you to help us stabilize our budget by your Christmas gift to our parish. ♛

This Monday at 7:30 p.m. we will have our Advent Penance Service. This begins with a prayer service featuring song, scripture, a homily and a review of many of the issues which constitute and contribute to our sins. The examination of conscience guides us to look at our lives with honesty, to realize what leads us to sin, and to deepen our trust in the power of the forgiveness which Jesus offers through the Church. Bishop John and several local priests will join the four of us here at Christ the King as we offer this sacrament of spiritual healing.

I often compare the Sacrament of Reconciliation to a physical check-up. It is wise to do both on a regular basis, in order to deal with any critical issue, to diagnose any emerging issue, to talk honestly about, to analyze and to develop a plan for dealing with problems, and to strengthen our resolve to live with wellness — both physical wellness and spiritual wellness.

The beauty of a Penance Prayer Service is that we are together. Among the people assembled at that service may be some people you have hurt, or at least some people you have disappointed or let down. By their presence they offer you their forgiveness and encouragement — just as you do the same for them. A Penance Service is a gathering of the Body of Christ; and as the Church, as the Body of Christ, we name our need for forgiveness and we offer to one another the encouragement and forgiveness we all need.

Many times we are helped on our spiritual journeys by going to confession to a priest we do not know and who does not know us. We feel a bit more free to bare our souls. And very often, one more set of priestly insights makes a big difference in our quest to change our lives and live more consistently in the light of Jesus.

We are a people on the journey towards welcoming Jesus into our hearts as we prepare for Christmas. Every Christmas is unique. Therefore, every Advent is unique. During Advent we focus on making the way straight for the Lord to come into our lives and into our world. Let us use this last week of Advent as a special time of prayer. Let us continue to pray for one another, let us pray for the children and youth of our community so that this Christmas will be a beautiful celebration of their love for Jesus, and let us pray for the folks we know who are motivated by this Advent season and by our celebration of Christmas to move to the next level in their dedication to live as vibrant disciples of Jesus. ♛

In these last days leading to Christmas, let us pray for the gift of inner peace. There will always be some last minute things to do; but let's make sure that we create space in our schedules so that our hearts are prepared to encounter Jesus. The depth of the way we welcome Jesus into our hearts sets the tone for the way we can be ambassadors for Jesus.

I recall the pilgrimage I made to the Holy Land in 1982. One afternoon our group went to Bethlehem and visited the chapel of the Nativity, which commemorated the birth of Jesus. The small chapel was filled with people; it was crowded, loud, there was little semblance of reverence. There was a large star on the floor, decorated in a somewhat garish way. It was too much! I departed quickly and went shopping; of course souvenir booths were all around. I went back to the chapel. It was empty. It was a beautiful time of prayer. If the star was not the exact spot, it was somewhere close by where Jesus came into the world. The overdone star now spoke of the extent to which we go as we try to express the inexpressible. Part two of the visit to the chapel was one of the highlights of the pilgrimage.

Many of us will revisit some memories of Midnight Mass and its power for us years ago; some of us have powerful memories of family times, times of joy, reunion, even reconciliation at Christmas-time. But not everyone's memory-bank is so rich that it nurtures inner peace.

As we live in the present moment we are able to prepare the way in these last few days leading to Christmas.

Pray with the songs of Christmas and Advent. Feel their faith, bask in their messages of hope, consolation, and love. Do a bit of research on the life situation of the composer at the time the song was developed.

Envision the joy that your Christmas gifts can bring. Revisit the love, affection and respect you have for those you are giving a gift to. Bring them to Jesus in your heart. Let your gift be an expression of gratitude. Take a second look at some of your Christmas cards and give thanks for the senders.

See Christmas through the eyes of small children...see Christmas through the love of parents of infants...see Christ through the eyes of small children...see Christ through the love of parents of infants.

Spend some time reflecting on the crèches at home, in church and in various places throughout the community. It is striking that as nativity sets are fashioned throughout the world, the Holy Family and the supporting cast of folks and critters are always representative of the particular nation and culture where the crèche has been crafted.

Take a drive and drink in the lights. It is not a contest to see who has the greatest display, but a reminder of He who has come as the Light of the World.

Read the scriptures, take an extra time in the Eucharistic Chapel, go to daily Mass, pray the rosary, pray for the poor, for refugees, for immigrants; take a walk in the arboretum, bake some cookies, take a nap...do something, give some time to these last days of Advent in order to prepare the way for the Lord Jesus to touch your life in a unique manner. ♛

During Advent, the Church guides us to prepare for the Coming of Jesus. The Church's Liturgy refers to the First Coming of Jesus and the Second Coming of Jesus.

The first coming of Jesus takes us to Bethlehem, as we give thanks for God taking on human flesh and being born as a baby to Mary and Joseph. In many ways we try to recreate the pilgrimage of Mary and Joseph to Bethlehem, their quest for a place to stay for the night, Jesus' being born in a manger, and being welcomed by shepherds and angels. It was a holy night when the world totally changed. God became one with humanity. The Word of God was made flesh and dwelt among us. The first coming of Jesus generates tender feelings for the Holy Family, but also gratitude for the great love of God.

The second coming refers us to the coming of Jesus at the end of the world. This time will be what is often called the Last Judgement, the separation of those who for all of eternity will be with God and those who will be living out the results of their radically sinful lives. The concept of the second coming has a bit of a "Lenten" feel, a call to repentance or conversion, a challenge to change our lives and to encourage others to do so. And yet, it also has a glorious element to it, as the second coming refers to the Ultimate Manifestation of Jesus at the time when the universe comes to an end.

During Advent, our most common church hymn is "Oh Come, Oh Come, Emmanuel". It has a yearning, plaintive mood as we sing with hope for the ways our God can come into our lives and our world. It is based on the ancient pre-Christian hope for God to send a Messiah who would bring freedom to the defeated and oppressed Jewish people. However, it also speaks to the liberation from the sin and self-centeredness which can so weaken personal and national character that threatening forces beyond and within can take over. The various verses of "Oh Come, Oh Come, Emmanuel" have their source in the psalms and are part of the Breviary readings for the last week of Advent. They are called the "O antiphons."

We ask for Jesus to come into our lives in many different ways. Very often our prayer of petition shifts from an appeal on our behalf for a specific cause to a humble request that Jesus just come to us. Jesus invites us to come and to follow him and his way. Jesus comes into our lives in every one of the sacraments, especially the Eucharist. As the last book of the Bible, the Book of Revelation concludes, the second last sentence is "Yes, I am coming soon!" Amen! Come Lord Jesus!

Jesus desires to come into our lives. Concurrently, one of the critical aspects of Christian faith is the human desire to come to Jesus and to humbly accept Jesus coming to us. In so doing, we do not define how Jesus is to be with us, but our faith leads us to open ourselves to the way Jesus wants to purify, unclutter and sanctify us. ♛

# CHAPTER 46

## *Thomas Merton/Gethsemani:*

BULLETIN — January 10, 2016

BULLETIN — October 1, 2017

BULLETIN — December 9, 2018

Next Monday, January 18, on the evening of Martin Luther King Day, Deacon Bill Grimes will present a program on *Thomas Merton: Critic, Prophet, and Spiritual Master* in rooms D & E of the Parish Life Center at 7 p.m. Deacon Bill was a novice at Gethsemani and was under the direction of Thomas Merton. Deacon Bill is the pastoral associate at St. Julie's Church in Owingsville, a physician's assistant, one of the founders of the Hope Clinic in Bath County, and has been on the faculty at U.K.'s Medical School.

Thomas Merton was a monk at Gethsemani Monastery, just south of Bardstown. Merton was a writer and spiritual guide who has touched countless lives by his many essays and over 50 books. He lived a fairly "secular" life until his conversion to the Catholic Church as a young man. After teaching for a short time at St. Bonaventure College in New York, he entered the monastery in 1941. His abbot realized Merton's talent and desire to write and so encouraged him. In 1948 Merton's autobiography, *The Seven Storey Mountain* was published and became a best seller and it is still a very popular book. In subsequent years, Thomas Merton wrote on many different social and spiritual topics. He has been a soul brother to many people in many walks of life. His writings address civil rights, nuclear weaponry, war and peace, ecumenism and Eastern religions. He was a confidant to religious leaders who were participants in the Second Vatican Council and also to many social activists. His life was a testimony that life in a monastery, and a life dedicated to prayer, need not preclude concern for and involvement in issues in the "real world". But his life also made the point that the best social activism comes from a foundation of contemplative prayer. Prayer and action support one another.

Thomas Merton died in 1968 in Bangkok, Thailand while on a mission to engage in dialogue about prayer and monasticism with spiritual leaders in Eastern religions. Biographies of Thomas Merton have looked at his life in a way which reveals his humanity and which suggests that he was a person who conversion continually evolved and deepened. A great part of the attraction that Thomas Merton has for so many people is that his pilgrimage validates our own spiritual journeys and offers direction and hope and the assurance that we are not alone in our struggles to continually grow. Thomas Merton was a contemporary of Martin Luther King. As we observe our national holiday focused on civil rights, it is fitting that we reflect a bit on Merton's contributions to the unity and integrity to which we are all called. I hope you can join us next Monday, January 18 at 7 p.m. in the Parish Life Center. ◼

I will be away this week for a time of retreat at the Monastery at Gethsemani, near Bardstown Kentucky. Priests, deacons, and religious are all expected to make an annual retreat in order to give some concentrated time to prayer. The policy for priests of the diocese of Lexington is to go on retreat with all the other priests one year, and then, the next year, we are free to choose the place and style of retreat that we feel will be most beneficial.

When we priests go on retreat together, we hear presentations by a retreat director on prayer and ministry, in addition to taking time for liturgical prayer and quiet prayer. A plus of this kind of retreat is that because we are all together, we can nurture our sense of fraternity and our collective vision as priests serving in a mission diocese.

On the other hand, a retreat at a place like Gethsemani offers the opportunity for more solitude, to be inspired by the monks, to enter into the rhythm of the monastic day, and to let the Spirit of God serve first and foremost as our Retreat Director.

The monastery makes a powerful impression when you round a bend on a Nelson county rural road. The monks basically live within a walled enclosure removed from the distractions many of us face. However, I am always struck by the paradox of the

*You will be in my prayers. Our sick parishioners, our emerging young families, our pastoral staff, our school, our Capital Campaign, and our many parish activities will be in my thoughts and prayers.*

monastic community's understanding of and compassion for what is going on in the world and the struggles that people face in their daily lives. In many ways, to go on retreat at Gethsemani's monastery is less an escape from reality and more an entrance into what is most real.

A retreat offers an opportunity for some needed rest, an opportunity for evaluating and planning our lives, and also an opportunity to wrestle with some personal issues, and even with God. Many people who have never been on a retreat worry that they will be bored...yet a retreat often moves all too quickly.

Retreats are an invitation to listen; to be quiet and listen, to wait for God's Word, to empty ourselves from our distractions and agendas, and to give our Gracious Lord space to come in.

I will take you with me as I go on retreat. You will be in my prayers. Our sick parishioners, our emerging young families, our pastoral staff, our school, our Capital Campaign, and our many parish activities will be in my thoughts and prayers. But even more so, I will be praying for the spiritual growth, the embrace of discipleship, and the walk with Jesus to which every parishioner is called. I ask that you keep me in your prayers as I go on retreat. ♛

Advent is a season of devotion to Mary. This Friday evening and Saturday afternoon we have celebrated the feast of her Immaculate Conception, Mary's life lived without sin, so pure and dedicated that she was free from the inclination to sin, from original sin, free from a feeling that sin could be attractive. On Saturday afternoon we have hosted Bishop John and the Diocesan Hispanic community as they have celebrated the great Mexican feast of Our Lady of Guadalupe. Our Church's sanctuary is adorned this weekend with the beautiful presentation of Our Lady of Guadalupe. This Wednesday is the actual feast of Our Lady of Guadalupe and our 8 a.m. Mass for the grade school will have a special Hispanic flavor as the school community pays homage to our beloved Mrs. Lopez.

On our prayerful pilgrimage through the Advent season, many of us will focus frequently on the faith of Mary, her tenderness, the love that she and Joseph shared, and their journey from Nazareth to Bethlehem. We can trust that many of the Hispanic people who have been part of the caravan to the U.S. border have been praying night and day, asking for Mary's guidance and protection.

This Monday, the Church commemorates the 50th anniversary of the death of Thomas Merton. Thomas Merton was a monk at the monastery of Gethsemani, located just a few miles south of Bardstown. The monastery is correctly named the Abbey of Our Lady of Gethsemani. That is quite a title.

We can imagine that Jesus felt the presence and prayers and faith of his mother as he prayed in the Garden of Gethsemani on the night before he died. Jesus had the Passover Meal with his apostles, he instituted the Eucharist and the Priesthood, and he taught the powerful lesson of foot washing. Then he went to the garden to pray and to wait for his betrayer to arrive and the subsequent apprehension. In the garden Jesus faced his worst fears, he faced whatever internal darkness was plaguing his spirit, and he gave himself entirely to the will of God.

In the woods surrounding the monastery of Gethsemani there are several different statues. The most famous are the statues of the Christ and the apostles in the garden. The three apostles who accompanied Jesus are portrayed as the Gospels portray them, asleep, unable or unwilling to be the men that Jesus needed them to be. And there is the statue of Jesus, full of anguish but also standing as the great man of faith that he is. It is such a powerful image that grown adults have been moved to embrace the statue in prayer. Not that far away from the Gethsemani statues is the statue of Our Lady of the Fields. Again, at the very least, the spirit of Our Lady of Gethsemani was with Jesus as he prayed on the night before he died.

Thomas Merton felt like the Blessed Virgin led him to become a monk and that she guided him through his life. As a monk, Merton focused his life on quiet prayer as a way to get to know God's will and dedicate himself to embracing and being embraced by God. At the monastery every day ends with night prayer, Compline, climaxing in the dark chapel as the monks and their guests walk silently to the front of the chapel, to be blessed by the abbot with holy water reminding them of their baptism into the life and death of Jesus. And at the head of the first pew is an icon of Mary, Our Lady of Gethsemani. ♔

# CHAPTER 47

*Our Lady of Guadalupe:*

BULLETIN — December 11, 2016

This Monday at 7 p.m., our cathedral will host a Diocesan-wide celebration of *Our Lady of Guadalupe*. This is a very special festival, not only for natives of Mexico, but also for all of us living in America, because the Virgin of Guadalupe is the patroness of the Americas. In our missionary diocese, in many parishes the number of baptisms of Hispanic children is basically the same as the number of baptisms of Anglo children. Latino Catholics make up a large percentage of Catholics in our diocesan territory. And so, on Monday evening, the Feast of Our Lady of Guadalupe Mass will be offered here at 7 p.m. by Bishop John. Hispanic Catholics from throughout the Diocese of Lexington will be in attendance.

Even if you do not speak one word of Spanish, I encourage you come; and I promise you an inspiring experience of God's Spirit at work.

Nuestra Señora de Guadalupe

The image of Our Lady of Guadalupe conveys a powerful message. The hill of Tepeyac (Guadalupe) was a sacred site for Aztec spirituality. There Mary appeared to a simple Native-American peasant, Juan Diego. Our Lady of Guadalupe is not fair-skinned, like the Conquistadors from Spain, but she is dark-skinned like an Indian, like a native of Mexico in the 16th century. Our Lady's blue mantle is covered with stars, and she is standing on a crescent moon held aloft by a peasant/angel — this presentation symbolizes a respect for the native Aztec culture and religion and conveyed the powerful message to Mexico's Native Americans of Mary's love for them. Our Lady of Guadalupe is portrayed as pregnant since she is giving birth not only to a people blending Spanish and Native American cultures who are soon to share in the same faith. As Mary spoke to her messenger, Juan Diego, her message was a strong message of respect for and solidarity with the poor and the oppressed.

In the 16th century, Mexican Native Americans had been resistant to the missionary efforts of the Church as the Church was so enmeshed in the dominative spirit of the Spanish invaders. Following Mary's appearance at Guadalupe, the Church's missionary approach became much more pastoral and the Native Americans became much more open to the church. Within six years of Mary's appearances at Guadalupe, nine million Aztecs were baptized!

Throughout the years, the Virgin of Guadalupe has become a central figure in Mexican spirituality and that of many other people who know the experiences of poverty and oppression. In this day and age, when there is much negative reaction to brothers and sisters who have come to the U.S. for a better chance at a stable life, Our Lady of Guadalupe speaks to all our hearts. ♛

# CHAPTER 48

*Christmas:*

BULLETIN — December 25, 2016

BULLETIN — December 22, 2019

On behalf of all of us on the pastoral staff I wish you a joyful and grace-filled celebration of Christmas, as we celebrate the love that God has for us. It is a love so great that Jesus entered into our world; Jesus was born as a human baby, in order to redeem us, in order to lead us to new life, in order to guide us so that we can live the fullness of life on this earth and beyond.

In the midst of all the special moments of this day, it is good to reflect on the spiritual meaning of the birth of Jesus and to draw from God's Biblical Word.

The Gospel of Luke describes the journey of Mary and Joseph to Bethlehem, how there was no place for the couple to stay the night in a comfortable manner, and how Jesus was born in a stable, in a manger. Shepherds, not kings or scholars, or religious leaders were the first to welcome Jesus. The message is that Jesus is one with the poor and the homeless, the peasant and the night-shift worker. And God's mysterious angels tell them and us that Jesus has come for all of us.

The Gospel of Matthew places Jesus as the culmination of a genealogy that includes men and women, saints and sinners, a genealogy which the Sacred Author crafted through Matthew's writing to convey that Jesus came as the fulfillment of Jewish history, and had the heritage of real people with their strengths and flaws. He was recognized by people of wisdom who did not share the Jewish religion but who so yearned to encounter God that they journeyed from the East to bring him gifts. And yet, Jesus was seen as such a threat by the ruling monarch that he mandated a mass murder of babies in order to kill Jesus. Matthew's nativity story tells us that Jesus will elicit extreme responses of joy and fear, of acceptance and rejection, of giving our life to him...and seeking to take his life.

> **Jesus has come as the LIGHT of the world. The LIGHT has come into the darkness, has pitched his tent next to the tents of the multitude of nomadic wanderers who symbolize all of humanity, and the Word became flesh and has dwelt among us...and the darkness will never overcome the LIGHT.**

John's Gospel does not take us to a historic moment in a place in Israel, but paints the mystical picture of Jesus, the Word of God, taking flesh. This is the same Word spoken at the beginning of creation when God said, "Let there be LIGHT". Jesus has come as the LIGHT of the world. The LIGHT has come into the darkness, has pitched his tent next to the tents of the multitude of nomadic wanderers who symbolize all of humanity, and the Word became flesh and has dwelt among us...and the darkness will never overcome the LIGHT.

And so, we who are blessed and needy, we who are young and old, we who are full of faith and a bit foggy, we all rejoice that God has so loved the world, that he sent his only begotten Son to guide us to live as people of the LIGHT.

We prepare for Christmas. We prepare to celebrate the great love that God has for us. Jesus is God who chooses to come into our world, into our lives, into our Church, into our homes. Jesus will teach us the way to live as he grows up in the home of Joseph and Mary, as he responds to the Holy Spirit guiding him through life, as he calls forth a band of disciples whom he shapes into apostles, as he engages in a ministry of healing and spiritual empowerment, as he clarifies and testifies to the truth, as he challenges the forces of sin and counters the abusive power of the establishment, as he faces fear and endures pain and gives his life, and as he fulfills the core human hope that death is not the end, but a new beginning.

Christmas leads us to admire Mary and Joseph...they are portrayed by people throughout the world as a man and woman of their own color and characteristics; the olive skinned Mary and Joseph encourage every one of us to open our hearts to the call of the Angel Gabriel and to honor the life of Jesus within us and in our midst. Mary and Joseph remind us that we are all pilgrims, we are all on a journey, we are all subject to secular powers who lead us to places and situations which are dangerous. Like Mary and Joseph, we all need safe places to rest, to

*Gerard van Honthorst*

call home, and to nurture life and faith. Mary and Joseph continue to travel in solidarity with our own existential wanderings, but they also accompany today's homeless, today's immigrants and refugees, and today's outsiders.

Christmas is the time of angels and shepherds. The angels welcome Jesus songs of joy and faith. From beyond the farthest galaxy they come...whether propelled by wings, singing and playing horns, arranged as Cherubim, Seraphim, Dominions, etc., we will never know, but eternal beings, full of life and full of faith and joy were present and added to the acknowledgement that history was changing. And their message is one of encouragement...advocating courage...do not be afraid. Jesus is Lord God...Jesus is with you...Jesus is King of the Universe and King of all peoples.

The shepherds represent all common folk, people like you and me, people just trying to do the best we can in our part of the world, in our time in history. A case can be made that they came to the manger with no idea of the enormity of the birth of this one child, but they came with their understanding of life, birth, life's vulnerability, and the preciousness of every life, and that they were transformed by the grace radiating from the newborn Messiah and from Joseph and Mary. Jesus came for the sophisticated and the ordinary people and his light was already shining in the darkness of fear, confusion and oppression.

On this Christmas let us recall the blessings and the challenges of our lives and give thanks for the presence of Jesus in good times and in bad. Let us also recall the blessings and the challenges of our world, our nation, our Church, and our cathedral parish...and the presence of Jesus Our Savior in every event, season and wonderment in our lives. That is God's ultimate present...let us give thanks for the presence of Jesus! 👑

# CHAPTER 49

*Beyond Christmas:*

BULLETIN — December 30, 2018

BULLETIN — December 29, 2019

BULLETIN — December 27, 2020

The days after Christmas which lead into today hurl us quickly past the tranquility of the manger scene in Bethlehem. Leaders of the Church over the centuries have designated certain days as feast days. I cannot help but think that the Holy Spirit often has inspired their sense of timing.

December 26, the very day after Christmas, is the feast of St. Stephen. Stephen was a deacon and the first martyr. His feast reminds us that there are times in our lives when we need to give our all, to dedicate our lives to the truth, to trust that God will give us the grace we need in order to face an ordeal. Because Jesus came into the world and has shared his life with us, countless men and women, over the ages have found the strength and courage to give their lives for the Good News of the redeeming love of Jesus. As Stephen was martyred, a man named Saul was present, holding the cloaks of those throwing stones at Stephen. One definition of a martyr is "one who gives witness." Saul who became St. Paul was affected by the witness of Stephen.

*St. John the Evangelist by Joan de Joanes*

The next day, December 27, is the feast of John the Evangelist. John's Gospel emphasizes that Jesus came as the light of the world, a world that has been steeped in darkness. Jesus is the Word of God, a creative word who became flesh and dwelt among us. John tells us that God so loved the world that he sent his only begotten Son. John's Gospel refers to the beloved disciple, possibly a reference to himself as the gospel writer, but probably a reference to all of us who are called to realize that we are all beloved by God. John, and the Johannine school of scripture writing, have a mystical sense, but also attest in an unparalleled manner that the coming of Jesus has changed the history of the world.

Friday, December 28 is the feast of the Holy Innocents. These are the baby boys killed by order of King Herod because he felt threatened by the newborn baby — Christ the King. He was so eager to be rid of Jesus that he decreed that all male babies recently born in Bethlehem and its vicinity should be slain. This feast is a revelation that even as Jesus came into the world, the darkness was fearful and rejected him. This sad day bears testimony to the negative power of insecurity.

On this weekend, we celebrate the feast of the Holy Family. We very often experience this weekend as less hectic than Christmas and the days leading to Christmas. And so we can savor the beautiful reality of Jesus being born into a human family. We can visualize Joseph helping Mary deliver Jesus, both of them holding Jesus, Joseph kissing his wife with joy, Mary feeding Jesus, Mary and Joseph singing and saying sweet words to Jesus as he would cry. And we share in the prayers of thanksgiving Mary and Joseph offered as they marveled at the little person they were already so in love with. We celebrate this weekend the ideals of family life, and also how our family lives can prepare us as adults to live in the light and to find and dedicate our lives to our mission in life. ◼

Today is the feast of the Holy Family. For many of us, it is a mellow Sunday when we can savor the blessings and the holiness of Christmas. I am away this weekend, visiting family and friends, and then taking a few days of retreat. My plan is to simply go to Mass this Sunday, and like you, to be part of a congregation — one of the visitors who will be welcomed.

Holy Family Sunday leads to reflections on our prime communities. We give thanks for our present families and our families of origin. We all have our stories of adventures, peak experiences, imperfections, forgiveness, reconciliation, and shared joy. As a parish we are called to be a community with many of the same qualities as a family. Religious communities of sisters, brothers, monks, seminarians, and even diocesan priests also have elements of family life. Family life and community life call on us to be givers. Let's try to give some special time this week to pray for our families, to pray for those who seek to nurture family life, and to offer encouragement to family members who are facing challenges and developments in their own lives.

When I was first ordained a priest in 1972, my first assignment was in Ashland, at Holy Family parish. Those were five wonderful years. Much of my ministry was serving as a teacher and guidance counselor in the parish high school, a school with about 100 students from ninth to 12th grades. In such a small school, all of us 10 faculty members did something we were not trained to do. The students knew one another very well; many of them had been in Holy Family School from first grade to 12th grade. Holy Family High School certainly had a "family feeling"; every student knew every other student; many of them are still best friends as adults.

In the early 1980s Holy Family High School closed; it had just become too small to provide a quality and affordable education. A year after I left Holy Family, the Church was destroyed in a fire. But a new and magnificent Church was built on that site. At the time I served in Ashland, it was one of Kentucky's most prosperous cities. Ashland Oil and Armco Steel employed many people and were highly successful businesses. Both have radically down-sized, have linked up with other companies, and have moved much of their operations. Ashland does not have the population and economy it once had, but both the city and the parish have adjusted to the changes. Let's hold Ashland's Holy Family parish in our prayers as they celebrate their parish feast day.

Today is also the feast day of Booneville's Holy Family Church. It is one of two parishes served by Fr. John Lijana. It is the only parish in Owsley County, one of the most impoverished counties in our nation. Two Franciscan Sisters reside in the parish and do outreach ministry and care for local people who are living in poverty. The parish itself has about 15 households. The small church is one of the gems of our Diocese's Appalachian ministry. It receives needed support from our Diocesan Annual Appeal.

We are all part of the family of the Diocese of Lexington. The funds generated by our Diocesan Annual Appeal support ministry throughout Eastern Kentucky. I encourage you to envision the ministry of the Church in both of our Holy Family Churches, and, if you have not yet done so, to make a generous donation or pledge to our Diocesan Annual Appeal. Both Holy Family parish communities are part of us — the Church Family of our diocese. ◼

One of my claims to fame within the Prabell family is that when we have our annual Christmas gathering and its accompanying sing-along, I am the designated "Five Golden Rings" voice when it is time for the "12 Days of Christmas." This is a year when our performance, if it takes place at all, will not be in-person. That is one more aspect of this year's Christmas season, when we are making choices to have less in-person contact and more choices to keep ourselves and everyone else safe.

And yet, the Twelves Days of Christmas is an ideal theme song for our unique journey through this season and our entrance into 2021. The Twelve Days of Christmas refers to the time frame from Christmas day itself to the traditional celebration of the Epiphany, on January 6. In this year when many of us have a more quiet and stay-at-home observance than usual, we need not sing or hum the tune multiple times, but we can savor the blessings of God loving us so much that Jesus came into the world as the humble babe born of Mary.

There are many great feast days during these 12 days, and this Sunday we celebrate the feast of the Holy Family. Beyond the history and the legends and theories of its meaning and the parodies about this Christmas carol, there is the central star of the carol: "My true love". My true love gave to me — and to all of us — his Only Begotten Son. God has given us so many gifts; God has blessed us in many ways. And God can be described as LOVE and defined as LOVE. God is our True Love.

Murillo

St. Paul in his first letter to the ancient Church in Corinth maintains that love is kind, patient, forgiving, rejoices at truth, and compassionate. And God is the source and the essence of all these qualities. In 1 John, 4:16 the sacred and inspired scripture tells us "We have come to know and to believe in the love God has for us. God is love, and he who abides in love abides in God, and God in him."

These 12 days can be a special time of entering into a spirit of love, as we connect with our families and friends in the best ways we can in these times when our options are limited. But we also draw from the depths of our hearts as we seek to be kind, patient, forgiving, truthful and compassionate. We ponder, we savor, and we choose to focus on our best memories.

During the 12 Days of Christmas the atmosphere of love leads to appreciation which leads to gratitude. I am very thankful for all the expressions of Christmas spirit and generosity which have been offered by you to our pastoral staff members and me. I am grateful for the special generosity at this time of the year as you give to our Church's needs and to charitable causes. I am grateful for all who rose to the occasion and helped our Christmas liturgies to be as beautiful, prayerful and as safe as they were. I am grateful for all who are making personal sacrifices so that we can prevail over the virus. And I am grateful for the love you have for our Church, for our faith, for our parish, for one another, and for our brothers and sisters who are living on the edge.

During these 12 Days of Christmas, I encourage us all to open our hearts a bit more to our True Love who has blessed us in so many ways. ▲

# CHAPTER 50

## *The Journey Towards Retirement:*

BULLETIN — March 14, 2021

BULLETIN — June 27, 2021

S everal parishioners have asked where I will be living upon retirement. I plan to be living in Lexington, in the Masterson Station subdivision, which is to the west of the city. The Diocese of Lexington owns six houses, three on one street and three on a parallel street; the backyards all run together; so it is like a small community. Each of the houses are one floor. Presently Fathers Nieberding, Osburg, and Curtis and Bishop John live in four of the houses; this summer, Fr. Terry Hoppenjans and I will move into the other two. Each member of the group lives independently, but gather daily for Mass and other community occasions. A moderate rent and other expenses are each priest's responsibility.

Several have asked what I will be doing. That is a tricky question for someone who has been doing a lot. So one aspect of the answer is "I will be doing less"...but I do intend to continue to serve. There is always a need for priests to substitute for another priest who is away or sick. I am fairly sure that I will find a few ministries in which I will invest myself, but it is too early to name what those will be. The best advice I have head about retirement is to avoid making too many commitments too quickly, and basically ease into things...to let the opportunities for engagement and ministry find you. I do look forward to continuing to minister without the responsibilities which are part of a position such as cathedral rector or pastor of any parish.

Some have asked, did you choose to retire or did a policy dictate that you needed to retire. By diocesan policy, a priest may retire at 70; in fact, he needs to submit a retirement letter to the bishop every year after his 70th birthday, but he can also state his openness to continuing in active ministry. I have for four years stated my openness and desire to continue at Christ the King. This year, I expressed my desire to retire and Bishop John has accepted that request.

Some people have said, you do not look like you are almost 75. I appreciate the compliment. However, I do have a few moderate health issues which could hamper my effectiveness if I would continue in this position or in any full-time assignment. I hope to address these in the time of retirement, but I also realize that getting older means getting older.

Some people have asked, will I be around Christ the King. There needs to have a balance on this one. It is important to give my successor space to serve you, so that you and he can get to know one another and work out the unique rector-congregation relationship into which the Spirit will lead you all. But it is also important to honor the friendships and connections we have forged over the years. So I hope to be available on the right occasions and to be supportive of the next steps which Christ the King and the new rector take together.

There are more questions about retirement than these, and some of the questions have less clear answers than those I have offered. I am appreciative of the questions you ask about my future and present life. They are expressions of your affection...plus opportunities for us to learn from one another how to regard retirement. It is an ending of course, but also a new beginning; among other things, for a Christian, it is a new avenue to find and to be found by God. ♛

Thank you for all the expressions of affection and gratitude for Father Damian and me as we are departing this week to enter new chapters in our ministries. The parish will be in good hands with Fathers John and David, our team of deacons and pastoral staff members, and all of you who live out your discipleship by means of your service to the mission of our parish. We all feel some concern that the priests' team will be two rather than three priests, but there will be several priests in the area who can be of assistance with Masses and Confessions. Plus, as always, the Holy Spirit has some wonderful surprises in store for us.

This is my last rector's column for our bulletin. It has regularly been part of my weekend prayer and reflection to write these. I hope that you have been able to find some inspiration, hope and guidance in these columns. In this final article, I will offer some thoughts on Jesus. I believe that all of us want to be closer to Jesus. When I reflect on the reasons for my life as a priest, an enduring response is that I am a priest in order to get closer to Jesus and to help others get closer to Jesus.

Jesus is a teacher who has taught by word and example. He balanced the law with the way of love. He developed his apostles so that they could share the Good News and change the world. Jesus taught the way of foot-washing. He taught us by his death that the way of faith and courage can be redemptive and that, even in dying, we can be givers. He is still teaching us and our world.

Jesus has been a healer. He cured the sick, raised the dead, and gave life to those whose spiritus had been deadened. In times of storms, he healed the earth. He healed those possessed by evil spirits, he forgave sinners, and he empowered ex-sinners to be great evangelizers. And he passed on his healing power to his successors and to the Church. He is still healing us and our world.

Jesus has been a man of prayer. He prayed with gratitude. He prayed for strength in times that were challenging. He prayed to know and follow the will of his Heavenly Father. He went away by himself to pray. He taught us to pray, not only by his example, but by the Lord's Prayer and by his adherence to and building on the prayer rituals of the established Jewish religion. He is still praying with and for us and our world.

Jesus is truly human. He learned carpentry from his father; he hung out with fishermen; he is the good shepherd. He experienced mountains, deserts, lakes,...but he also experienced temptations and every human emotion. Jesus lived with humility and integrity. He had friends. He was devoted to his mother. He saw the potential for good in every person. He cared for the poor, the vulnerable, the rejected, and those who rejected him. He is still our best friend.

Jesus is a visionary. He instituted the Eucharist so that we can be regularly nourished by his very person. He sent the Holy Spirit upon the apostles so that they could draw from his Spirit and thus transformed to share the Good News in a way that would be inspiring and solid. He has sent the Holy Spirit to guide the development of the Seven Sacraments and to guide the Church during its development in all the seasons of its life. His vision has guided the Church as we have needed to make changes, as we have needed to repent, as we have sought to build and re-build our communities and spirit. This vision continues to be the Light that shines in the darkness.

And so, brothers and sisters...may God bless you with the fullness of a life embracing and being embraced by Jesus. ...amen...alleluia. ♔

# AFTERWORD

There is an art to being retired. I am no expert. I have been at it now for about nine months, many of which have been months of limited social circulation because of Covid protocols. Retirement experts speak of the first year or so being a time of adjustments, surprises and some stress. I would not disagree. But like all of life, retirement is a time of grace.

I am very grateful for my new home. I live in a small house in Masterson Station. It is comfortable and moderately expressive of my personality. Many of the amenities that make my life comfortable and interesting are due to the generosity of Christ the King parishioners and the Diocese of Lexington. I am grateful to be living in a small community of five other retired priests. We each have our own house, we share one big back yard (or field), we have Mass together every morning, we go out to supper weekly, we watch out for one another, we share stories from our past lives, we compare our health concerns and the challenges of life in the world of technology, and in our own ways, we help one another to live with faith, hope and love. We are old and aging guys, but we are also brothers. All together, we have had over 300 years of ministry as priests!

When people ask me what I am doing, I say I am often helping at parishes with weekend Masses, have the Monday morning Mass at Lexington Catholic High School, serve as the priest chaplain at St. Joseph Hospital on Wednesdays, coordinate our team of four priests who offer weekly Masses at the Federal prison, and serve on the Board of Catholic Charities. I do a bit of spiritual direction and an occasional funeral, baptism and wedding. Additionally, I swim three times a week and also do some gym time.

People say that this sounds like a lot. However, I still have plenty of time for other pursuits and for just being. BEING includes availability to my family and giving more time and energy to God and daily prayer. The retirement lifestyle precludes the challenges of administration and all the duties and occasional stresses of serving as a pastor. Most of the time I do not set an alarm clock and sleep till I wake up.

Such is life. We are so much more than what we do. Retirement frees us to enter into the joy and the mystery of life and to feel the hand of God stirring the mix of our past, present and future. Our past can be full of regrets, mistakes and bad decisions; but it is also full of blessings, accomplishments and good decisions. Retirement frees us to put it all in perspective in the light of grace, to remember with gratitude, to quietly savor the lessons learned.

The future can be full of fears and the anticipation of loss, but it also opens the door for us to put our lives in God's hands and to trust that God really, really loves us ... right now and forever.

But most of all, retirement is an opportunity to live day by day in the present moment. Every day is a blessing ... every day is an opportunity. Retirement means we really have nothing we absolutely need to do, we have nothing to prove, we are not a thing ... not our work, not our buildings, not our bodies, not our trophies, not our writings, not our bucket list ... we are not any THING ... we are people loved by God and trying to let God come into our lives even more deeply and trying to love God and others more. That is why God made us.

*Father Paul Prabell*

Made in the USA North Chelmsford, MA
1318555_9798811643318
06.15.2022 0838